PALMETTO BRAIDING AND WEAVING

First publication, 1947

Cover basket by Susan Parke-Sutherland
Cover photography and design by Adrienne Nunez,
Echo Point Books & Media

ISBN: 978-1-62654-985-2

Published by Echo Point Books & Media
www.EchoPointBooks.com

Printed in the U.S.A.

Palmetto
Braiding and Weaving

Using Palm Fronds to Create Baskets, Bags, Hats & More

Viva Cooke & Julia Sampley

E P B M
ECHO POINT BOOKS & MEDIA, LLC

The supplies needed to complete the projects included in *Palmetto Braiding and Weaving* may be found in your own backyard, but if not, try your local craft supplier or one of these online stores:

www.basketmakerscatalog.com
www.hardypalmtrees.com
www.save-on-crafts.com

CONTENTS

INTRODUCTION

PALMETTO, palm, and straw braiding is an art as old as history, the skill being perpetuated, as is most frequently the case in native crafts, by home or word-of-mouth teaching from mother to daughter. It was in this manner the patterns recorded here were obtained and carefully written down so this old art might never be lost.

The very names of the patterns have a primitive, rustic flavor: *close-curl, fishtail, goose-eye, fishpot*—the latter a weave copied from that used in the construction of fish traps.

So far as we have been able to learn, no real effort has been made to collect and write the instructions for the various patterns which are the product of centuries of braiding. Occasionally a pattern was the result of a happy accident, but most of them bear the earmarks of patient planning. As one pupil so happily described a complicated braiding process: "It is like geometry; if one takes every step correctly the right answer is inevitable."

The braiding art was at one time practiced throughout the country, the material employed being that near at hand. In the grain-growing sections, grain straws were used; in other sections, grasses, rushes, and sedges. In the coastal plains and west-coast area where palms and palmettos grow, the fronds of these were used. In 1846, The Boston Almanac listed five firms importing palm leaves for making hat braids.

The palmetto craft is still practiced to some extent and many old timers argue the best means of harvesting, curing, and braiding. It was a flourishing industry in the early seventies and sustained many a "cracker" family. While the instructions in this book deal especially with the Sabal or cabbage palm, any palmetto or palm may be used, as well as many other materials. The cabbage palm is native to the southern United States, growing along the coastal region from Louisiana around the Gulf Coast to Florida and as far north as North Carolina. The decaying leaf stalks cling to the tree for many years and are spoken of as "boots"—thus the reference, "the tree that wears boots." The deeply cut, fan-shaped leaves are a shiny, deep green color and reach a maximum length of five to eight feet and of somewhat greater breadth. Careful harvesting of the next to the bud leaf does not injure the tree.

No record of dyeing the palmetto in the earlier days has yet been unearthed, but it is now possible to obtain an assortment of colors.

The collection of these patterns has been an absorbing hobby for us. Every braider of community note has been eagerly questioned and every new braid pattern considered a trophy!

Many have been helpful, to all of whom we are grateful, but appreciation is especially due to Mrs. C. P. Honeywell, Mrs. M. A. Tremiere, Mrs. H. L. Smith, Mrs. Ida Harrell, and Mrs. Nora Bashand, who have contributed so largely to both the pattern collection and to the palmetto lore.

MATERIALS

The use of native materials enhances the pleasure of all craftsmen, and, while the braids and articles in this book are made of palm or palmetto fronds for the most part, a little experimenting with native materials close at hand will produce excellent results. Toughness, length, and flatness are desirable, but many round-stemmed or -leaved rushes, sedges, grasses, and straws may be substituted for the palm fronds by simply flattening with the thumb and forefinger or by splitting the stems. Some of the straws, such as wheat, rye, oat, barley, and rice, may be flattened by this method and the size of the weaver or strand is naturally taken care of without splitting. Such material gives a glossy appearance to both sides of the braid. A variety and a pattern may be obtained by splitting these straws; the result—a braid in dull and bright tones. This applies to all round-stemmed or -leaved plants.

In 1864, the October issue of *Harper's New Monthly Magazine* tells of "Straw Bonnet" manufacture as a new industry in New England, using rye straw. It was begun in 1798 by Miss Betsy Metcalf of Providence, Rhode Island, who copied the braid she saw in a hat in a shop window. Miss Metcalf used oat stubble from her father's field. She taught others and the art spread from a little girl's desire for a straw bonnet to a thriving industry.

Corn shucks are quite suitable for braids, and splints of soft and hard woods may be used for the flat articles. Some split barks and roots may be used for braiding, but these materials are not common.

Frederick Leroy Sargent, assistant in the Botanical Museum of Harvard University, author of *Plants and Their Uses*, says, "Plaiting [braiding] consists of flat, fibrous strands sufficiently pliable to be folded into plaits or flat braids and used for straw hats, fine basketry, and the like." Keeping this in mind and knowing the pleasure derived from experimenting with new materials, the craftworker may discover many unusual, natural sources of beautiful materials suitable for use with these instructions.

For those unable to seek native materials, handicraft supply houses can furnish natural and dyed palm or palmetto frond and rush material ready for use.

Native materials should be cured or

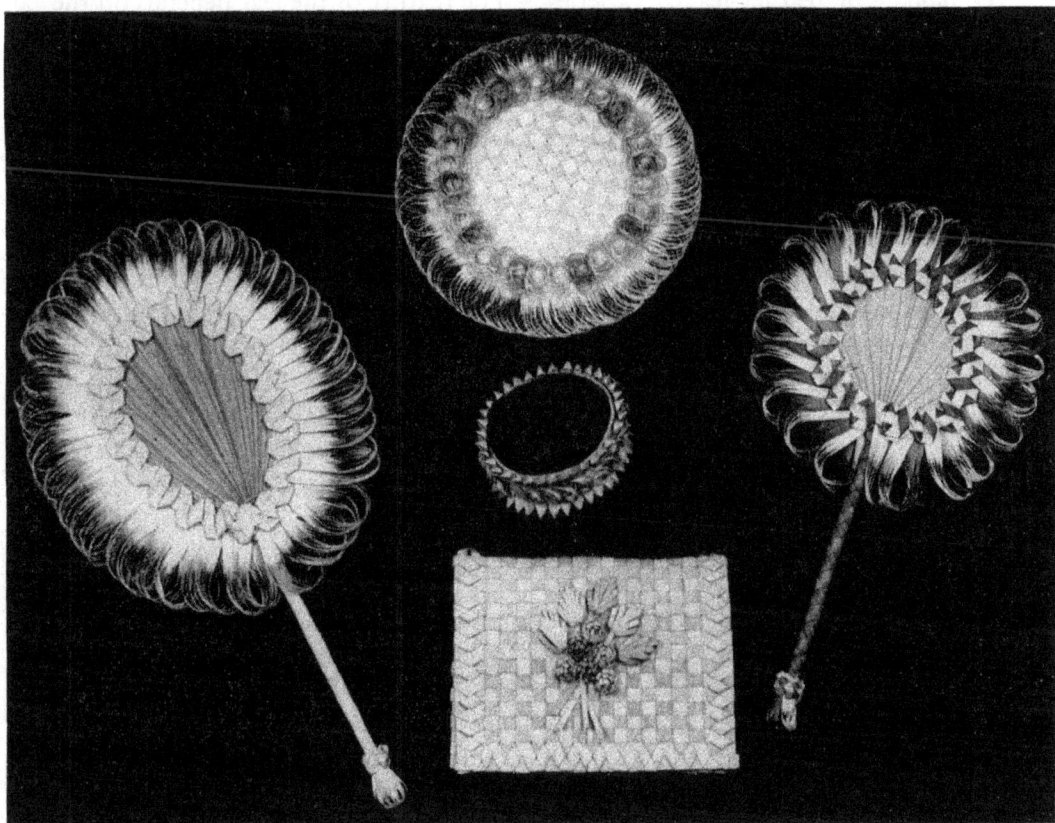

FIGURE 1. Styles of the eighteen-seventies, "pretty and fanciful." *a*. Fans of scrub palmetto trimmed with shredded palmetto. *b*. Pincushion of palmetto fiber, with side made of braided palmetto and shredded palmetto. (Center of picture.) *c*. Round mat made of check weave trimmed with shredded palmetto. *d*. Purse of check weave, trimmed with palmetto roses of push-and-pull trimming braid.

dried to allow for shrinkage, then soaked or wetted to make them pliable. Care should be taken to prevent too great an absorption of water, as this will cause the finished product to be loosely woven after shrinkage from drying. Strive for a firmly woven finished product. A good rule to follow is to wet the material thoroughly, leaving it in the water ten to fifteen minutes, then shake out the surplus water, roll the material in a heavy cloth, and leave several hours or overnight. The cloth will absorb the extra moisture and will give an even dampness to the material.

PALMS AND PALMETTOS

Palmate or fan-leaved varieties produce longer weavers, though many of the pinnate or feather-leaved varieties are suitable.

FAN-LEAVED PALMS OR PALMETTOS: *Cabbage*—Southeast United States; *blue-stem* or *dwarf*—Southeast United States along the coast Texas to Florida to North Carolina and in Arkansas; *Sabal Deeringiana* (delta-palmetto, palmetto-with-a-stem), native to southern Louisiana, along the lower Mississippi River, bayous, and lakes; *Sabal Texana*—Texas and Mexico; *needle palm*—Southeast United States; *saw or scrub palmetto*—from North Carolina and Arkansas, coastal plains area, Texas to Florida to South Carolina; *Washingtonia filfiera*—native to California, southwest Arizona, and borders of Colorado desert, cultivated in some southern states. In addition to these there are several varieties of palm native to Florida and many cultivated in southern and western states which may be used. All of the fan-leaved palms and palmettos should be gathered and cured as instructed in the chapter on the preparation of raw material.

PINNATE OR FEATHER-LEAVED PALMS: The *coconut palm*, native to Florida, is perhaps the best of this class, as its fronds are longer than other varieties. Any of the pinnate leaved palms with fairly long fronds are suitable. Among these are *royal*, *Alexander's*, *Cocos plumosa*, *sugar*, and *Arikury palm*.

Another harvesting method is used here. The full-grown, outside leaves, either allowed to cure on the tree or cut green and dried in the shade, should be used instead of the bud leaf.

The texture of the leaf depends on the type of palm. (Bleaching in some cases would probably be necessary if the product were dyed.)

The coconut frond, if allowed to dry on the tree, cures to a beautiful, dark brown color. The leaf may be harvested when the fronds turn yellow and the curing finished indoors. If cut green and cured the result is a soft, gray-green color. This material in either case is soft and pliable. The wetting, stripping, and use of the material is the same as for the fan-leaved variety.

YUCCA

There are many species of Yucca which occur in the United States. Among those best suited for this work would appear to be the *Spanish dagger*—North Carolina to Southern Florida and westward to Eastern Louisiana; *Spanish bayonet*—South-Central Texas to Northwestern New Mexico; *Schott's yucca*—Southern Arizona to Mexico; *Mohave yucca*—ranging in the Mohave desert, Southern Nevada, Western Arizona, and Southern California. These are suggested because of the length of the leaves. There are undoubtedly others.

The leaves and leaf fibers of these plants were an important material to the Indians for basketry. It is suggested the young leaves near the top be used for finer braids, while the coarser leaves may be used for coarse weaves of baskets and mats. The fibers may be used for sewing in coiled basketry. These leaves are thicker than

FIGURE 2. Shopping basket made of seven-strand check weave using the full width or un-split cattail leaf. It was used about six months by an itinerant teacher as a notebook and supplies carrier. Construction is the same as the eleven-strand herringbone shopping bag, Figure 16.

a   b   c

FIGURE 3-*a*. Braid in herringbone weave of leaf of cattail rush. A sturdy braid in tones of soft green and tan. *b*. Braid in lace-edge, hat-braid pattern of sheath of cattail leaf—the part of the leaf which grows under water. This is a soft, pliable material in lovely brown and tan tones. *c*. Braid in combination hat braid of bear grass (X-*Tenax*). Material is so pliable, can be worked without dampening.

the palm frond. By splitting off the fleshier part of the back of the leaf, a thin, strong material is left, which may be bleached and dyed or used natural. In harvesting, care should be taken not to bruise the leaves, as this sometimes causes dark spots. If the leaves are split, almost any pattern in this book is adaptable, and the fiber is strong and even, though the weavers are not long. The inner part of the split leaf will more readily take the dye, and therefore the pattern will be of light and dark shades. The splitting should be done when the leaf is partially dry or dry. Follow instructions in preparation of material.

RUSHES, SEDGES

There are many species of these families which are suitable for these instructions. A few will be named here, but the worker may discover many others near at hand. Any smooth stem or leaf of fairly strong fiber of fairly good length may be used—split for the finer work and used whole for coarser work.

BULLRUSH OR CLUB RUSH—marshes throughout North America; *soft or rice rush*—swamps and low ground throughout the United States; *black or brown rush*—brackish marshes, New Jersey to Florida and Texas; *hemp or wire-grass rush*—low ground throughout the United States; *chair-maker's rush*—(triangular stem) throughout North America. There are countless others suitable.

CATTAIL RUSH—marshes throughout North America. The finer leaves or thinner part of the larger leaves may be used for the finer braids. This is ideal material for articles made of the plain braids—either check or herringbone weave. Fig. 3-*a-b*. See the shopping bag, Fig. 2. A halo hat made of five-strand, check-weave braid, using the flat part of the leaf, was quite satisfactory. A ladies' handbag woven over a form was attractive. It is splendid for basketmaking over forms or dummies and cannot be beaten for rush-seating chairs. Beautiful and serviceable rugs may be woven on hand looms using cotton warp and cattail leaves as weft.

In gathering and curing rush or cattail, care must be exercised in handling. If bent while green, a break will occur in the dried material causing difficulties in working. Most of these should be gathered when the tip of the leaf or the tuft at the tip of the stem begins to turn brown. These should be cured in the shade, but must be turned frequently to prevent mildew or mold, unless they are laid on a slatted surface or a section of poultry wire for a good circulation of air.

Use the smaller rushes for the finer work. All round rushes may be split, the pith removed, and the rush split to uniform widths for braiding. Keep in mind, however, the change in tone of all split material, as in most cases the inner side will be dull or lighter in shade, while the outside will be bright and shiny. The difference will be particularly noticeable when the material is dyed. The bright-and-dull or light-and-dark patterns, however, will prove attractive.

PREPARATION FOR USING RUSH AND CATTAIL

The wetting is the same as for palmetto. If the leaf is used whole, as is most practical, each rush or cattail leaf should be wiped downward from tip to butt with a wet cloth to clean, redampen, and get rid of the air in the rush or leaf as it is used. Unless this is done carefully, shrinkage takes place and makes the work loose, unattractive, and unsubstantial. Do not work rushes or cattail leaves too damp; they should be only sufficiently damp to make them pliable. An excellent method of dampening is to leave them in the rain or under a lawn sprinkler for a short time the night before they are to be used, then wrap them in a heavy cloth for mellowing overnight.

SQUAW, BEAR, WHITE GRASS, AND TURKEY'S BEARD

Occur throughout North America. The long, tough, grasslike, lustrous leaves may be used natural or dyed. The center leaves are white or nearly so. They were commonly used by the Indians as the white pattern in their baskets, and leaves cut to uniform width were used as the weft of their gaudily dyed, flexible baskets.

The soft, fine center leaves should be suited to any braid pattern given, Fig. 3-c. The coarser outer leaves should be used for the sturdier braids and articles. It may be cured either in sun or shade, but if sun cured, care should be taken not to overcure, as it will become too dry and turn yellow and brittle. If leaves appear soft enough after curing, they may be used without wetting; otherwise prepare as in work with palm leaves.

GRASS, GRAIN STRAWS

Any stem or leaf of fairly good length, strong enough fiber to bear some strain and of at least one-eighth inch width is suitable. Either flatten the stems by pulling between tightly pressed thumb and forefinger when damp or split the stems. Leaves should be handled the same as palm fronds. Wherever possible choose the longest stems between nodes or joints so as to minimize splicing weavers.

Among the grasses are *sweet vernal* and *June grass* (these have been used in weaving imitation leghorn hats, using the whole stem flattened); *black oat grass* (use leaves); *manna, beach, brome, and tufted-hair grass*. Oat, Fig. 4-a, *wheat* Fig. 4-b, *rye, barley,* and *rice* straw are made suitable by either flattening or splitting the stems. Many of the leaves of the longer-leaved grasses are good, such as *gamma*, Fig. 4-c, *slough*, Fig. 4-d, and the *sorghums*. Most of the grass leaves should be allowed to mature thoroughly before harvesting. Whenever leaves are used, follow preparation of the material as given for palm leaves. Where stems are used whole, the nodes or joints are cut off and the lengths are sorted according to diameter in order to have even weaving strands. These are placed in water for ten to fifteen minutes. Then follow the procedure for wetting palmetto. Before braiding, take a cloth and wipe down each weaver, cleaning and removing excess moisture and air. Take care not to have the material too wet, as shrinkage will occur and spoil the effect. Straws and grasses may be bleached and dyed.

CORN SHUCKS

These are suitable for nearly all of the articles or patterns listed. They are very soft and may need wiring or linings for support of some finished articles. Corn shucks should be carefully selected for length. The inside leaves are softer and will cure a lovely white. These take dye readily. They should be worked damp, taking care not to allow to mildew. Follow general directions as in the chapter on preparation of materials.

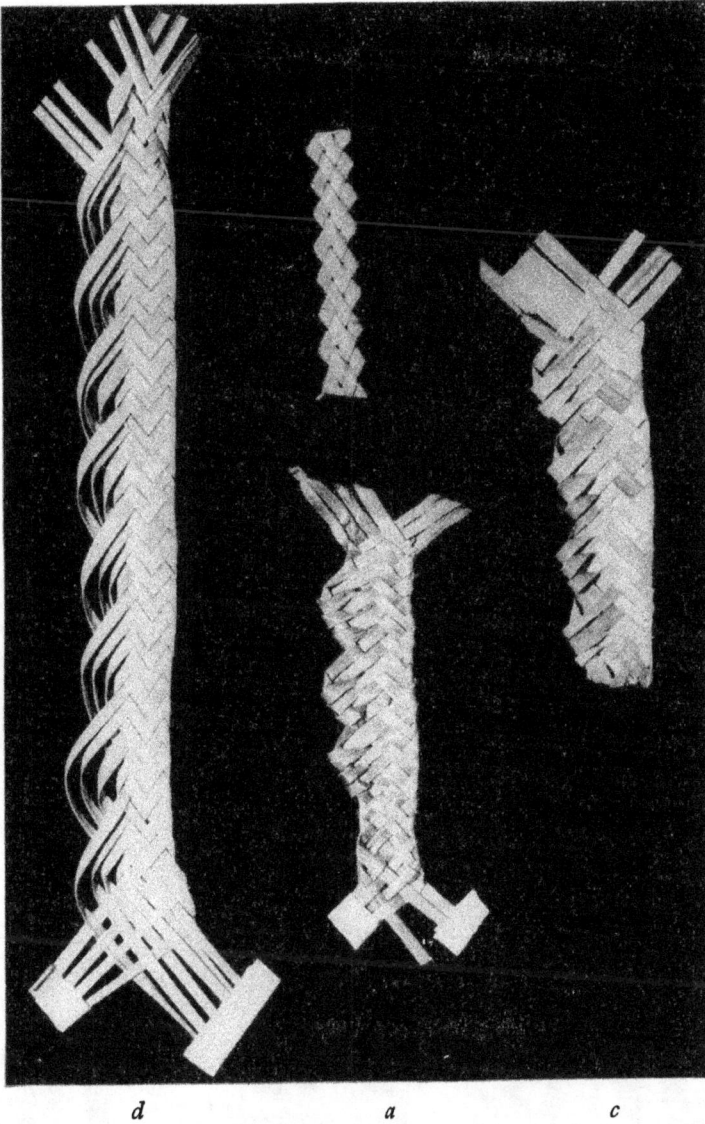

FIGURE 4-*a*. Braid of oat straw in pattern of graduated curl scallop in herringbone weave. This braid has a lovely, golden brown color, very glossy. *b*. Four-strand, fishtail-braid pattern in wheat straw. This sample was cut from a length of braid made before the Civil War. It is still lovely in color, glossy, and as sturdy as when first braided. *c*. Braid made of leaves of gamma grass, harvested after it had cured on the stalk, and, while not as tough as some of the other fibers, makes a fairly sturdy braid in varying shades of brown. This is the graduated curl scallop in herringbone weave. *d*. Leaves of slough grass from Kansas, woven in the lace braid with overlapping scallops, herringbone base. This grass cured to a lovely shade of light, soft green. While the leaves involute in drying, dampening them makes them flat and suitable for braiding. A sturdy, beautiful braid.

15

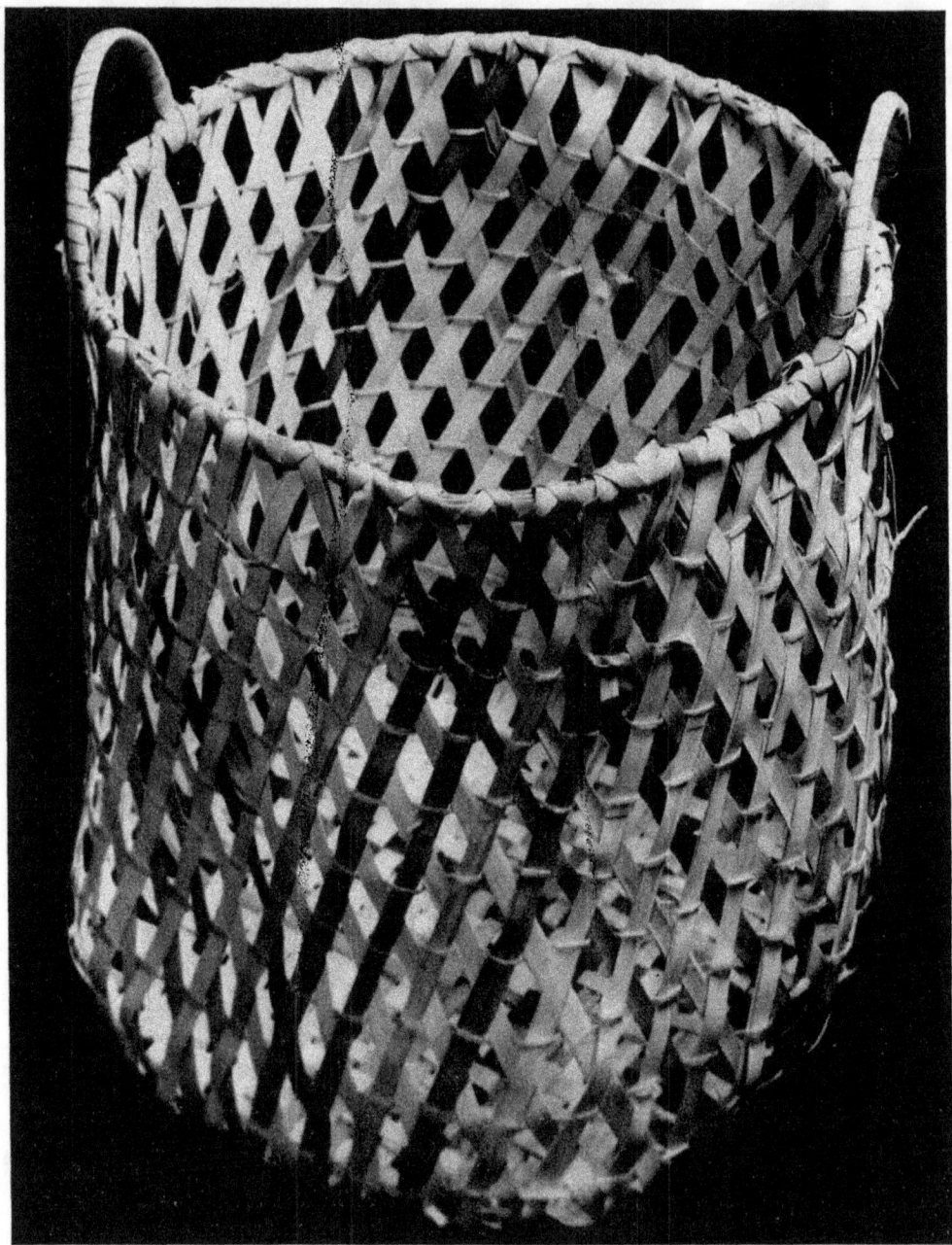

FIGURE 5. Basket of palmetto with horizontal weavers of mulberry root. Mulberry root is a strong, pliant fiber especially adaptable to basketry. This is a variation of the fishpot weave, beginning with the check weave on the bottom.

16

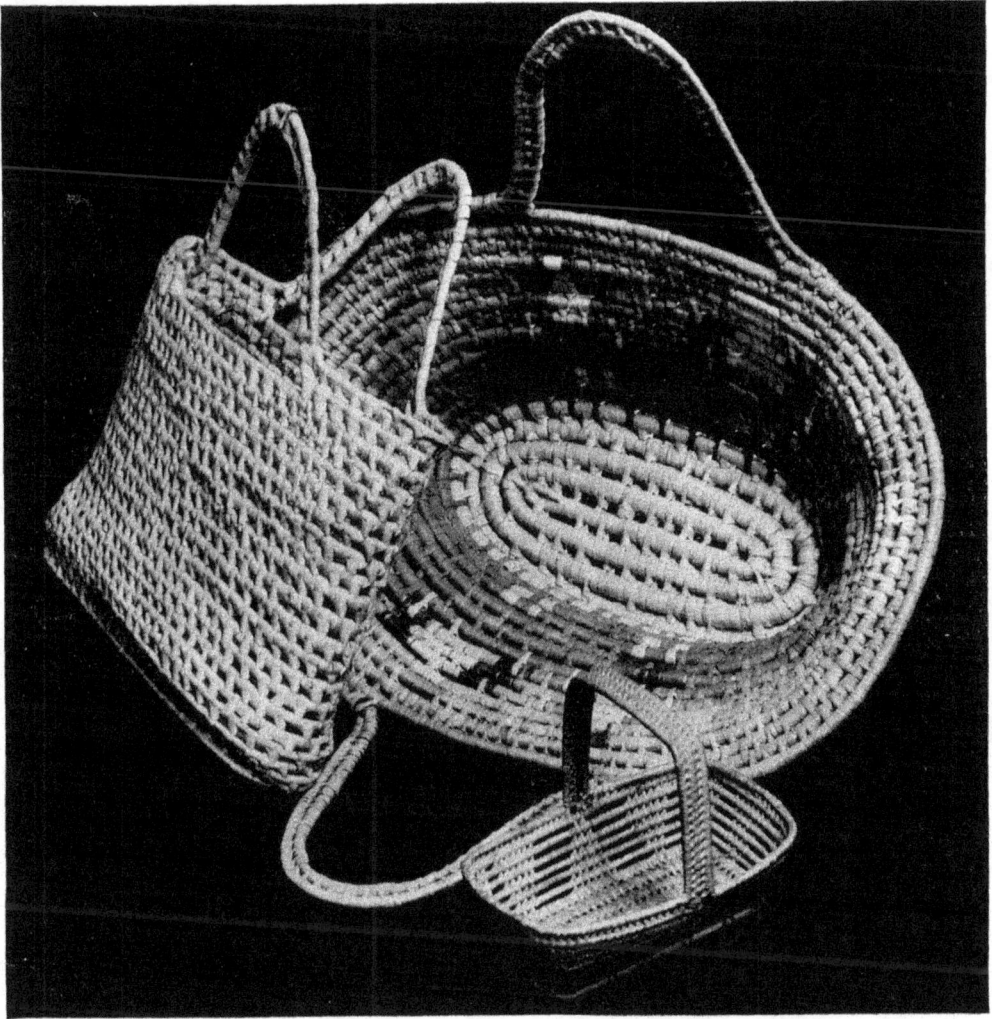

a   b   c

FIGURE 6-a. Shopping bag in coil weave. Effective, sturdy, and useful. Many materials are adaptable to this purpose. b. Large basket in coil weave of dyed palmetto. The colored weavers create patterns. Cattail and other materials may be used in this manner. Squaw or bear grass would be particularly good. Corn shucks and yucca, mulberry, and other roots and barks are suitable to this type of weaving. c. A key basket used many years ago in the South for carrying keys of the plantation household and storage rooms.

GENERAL SUGGESTIONS

The ingenious craftworker will devise a gauge knife to split weavers or strands evenly from these wider materials.

Decoration may be achieved on the articles by embroidering them with dyed raffia, mulberry root, and corn shucks. Basswood bark might be adaptable for this also. Mulberry root is splendid for basketry. Fig. 5.

Some of the plain braids may be enhanced by "inlaying," *i.e.*, by weaving colored strands into the finished natural braid by simply slipping a small piece or strand of the desired color over and under the woven strands following the pattern of the weaving.

COILED BASKETRY

Palmetto or palm fronds may be used as a binder or sewing medium instead of raffia for coiled baskets and mats, using as coils pine needles, wire grass, or the coarse ribs of the palm leaf. Patterns may be achieved with ease and the effort is quite worth while. The stitches can be spaced or may be worked solid. Fig. *6-a-b-c* shows examples of finished work.

COVERED BOTTLES

Bottles or vases may be covered solidly, using the regular pairing weave or a decorative covering in one of the flat, open weaves contained in any regular basketry instructions.

Chapter I

PREPARATION OF MATERIAL

HARVESTING AND CURING

THE leaf next to the bud leaf of the palm should be cut as soon as two or three inches of the stem shows above the wrapper or boot. (Cutting this second leaf from the tree does not injure the palm.) At this time in its development, the leaf is folded tight and pressed against the bud leaf, with no green except on the edges of the fronds. The best practice, from the authors' own experience, is to gather at the dark of the moon. A slight pull against both leaves will separate them from each other and the longer leaf, with a short bit of stem showing, may be cut just below the bottom of the fronds. Bend this tightly compressed, sword-shaped leaf outward and cut just over the arc of the stem. The fibers are taut from the bend and the leaf is easily cut, even with a light-weight penknife.

The fronds of the leaf should be torn apart along the folds, leaving the ends attached to the stem. Separate the fronds entirely to the mid-rib as they brown if not exposed to the air. Hang the leaf, stem up, in a protected place out of the sun but where a good circulation of air can reach it. It is not necessary to separate into half fronds, as curing is accomplished acceptably with the fronds separated at the shorter divisions only.

The cabbage palm or palmetto is best adapted for braiding. It cures a creamy white when harvested and handled properly and has a very satisfactory length which holds the need of splicing to a minimum. Also, it dyes well. There are, under ideal conditions of moisture and fertility, according to old settlers, thirteen leaves a year—one every moon—so the palmetto furnishes a year-round crop. However, the spring leaves are both heavier and longer. With favorable weather, the "cabbage fans," as the oldtime braiders speak of them, should be ready for use in two weeks, three at most.

There are those of the old braiders who insist on sun curing with dew moistening, claiming that the sun is a bleaching agent, and while this claim is true, the benefit is offset by the fact that the sun makes the product brittle. There are also advocates of an occasional salt-water dip during the drying period to toughen the fiber. There are those, too, of the old school who

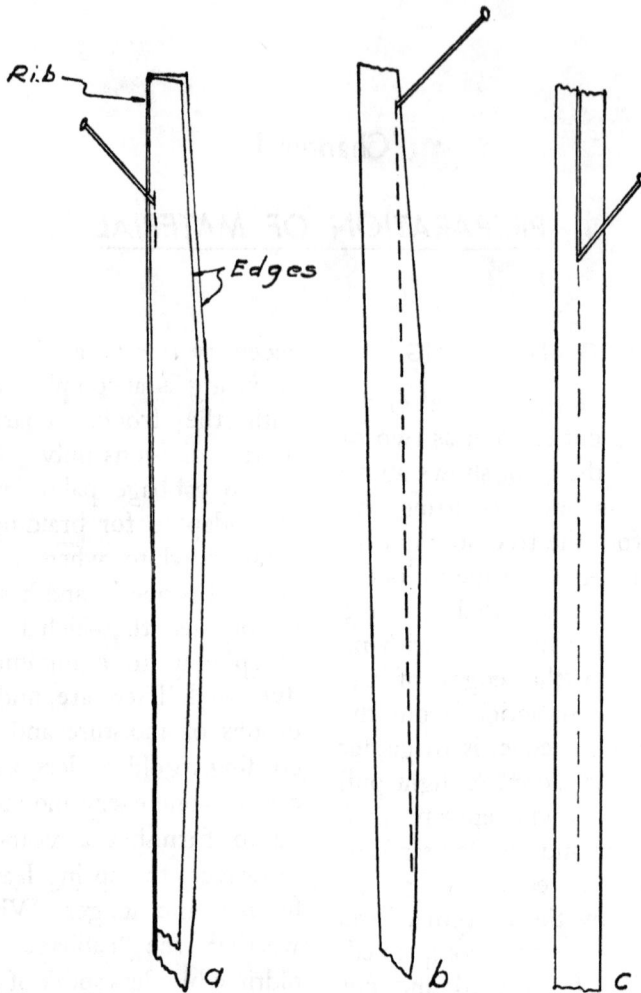

FIGURE 7-*a*. The full frond of palmetto, with a pin stuck in between the leaf parts and the rib. This pin strips the rib off closely, leaving two sections of the frond. *b*. The manner in which the edges are now stripped from the sides of both frond sections. Start stripping the edges at the butt or stem end of the frond. *c*. The frond being stripped to size strand required for the pattern or object to be made. NOTE: When palmetto fronds are supplied by handicraft-supply houses, steps shown in *a* and *b* are eliminated.

prefer to work with the saw or scrub palmetto, saying the material is softer, a fact which cannot be gainsaid, but the short fronds make constant splicing necessary and the product will not hold its bleach but, with time, turns a pinkish gray; nor will the braided article stand wetting without darkening.

NOTE: It is best to keep the fans hanging. If they are piled on each other or are packed away where air cannot get to them, they are inclined to mold and mildew.

STRIPPING

The evening before the product is to be used, the desired quantity of fronds should be cut from the stem of the dried leaf and the ribs or edges removed by sticking a pin in the frond behind the rib on the straight side at the butt or stem end, Fig. 7-*a*, and stripping to the tapering end, thus dividing a frond into two parts. The usual half of a frond will give about three strips (two long and one shorter) about one-quarter inch wide, depending, of course, on the width of the frond. The pin, drawn down the leaf,

follows the fiber of the frond and splits it easily and cleanly. Fig. 7-*b*-*c*. Do not discard these strippings. They make good material for coiled baskets, slippers, shopping bags, mats—wherever a coil material is required.

WETTING AND MELLOWING

Long soaking waterlogs the palmetto, causing undue expansion and consequent shrinkage, which results in an unsightly, open braid. The strips should be soaked in water for one-quarter hour only, then wrapped in a heavy, wet cloth or paper for mellowing overnight and be taken from this wrapping only as needed by the progress of the braiding. Each color should be soaked in a separate container and wrapped separately.

In ordinary weather (not unduly hot), the wetted palmetto may be held over the second day without souring. After that time, if there are mellowed strips yet unused, they should be laid out to dry. Palmetto may be wetted and dried any number of times, but care must be taken to dry it out before fermentation sets up.

Chapter II

BRAIDING

PROCEDURE

There are two basic weaves, check and herringbone, of which the check weave is the simpler.

Of the check weave, there are two divisions—the uneven or odd-number strand weave and the even-number strand weave. The uneven-number weave is the simplest of all braids, so we use it to teach procedure, hold, tightening, splicing, and for practice in developing a technique.

RULE I. *In all uneven-number strand braids the edge strands turn over— that is, to the top.*

Regardless of how many strands are used, if the number is uneven, the procedure is exactly the same; the edge strands turn up and are woven over one, under one, to the center of the braid. Work on alternate sides and always on the side that has the greater number of strands. For instance, in a five-strand braid, weave the side that has three strands. When this is done, the opposite side will have three strands.

POSITION OF HANDS IN BRAIDING

Hold so as to braid from you. This is essential, as it makes tightening of the braid easy and also makes for efficiency and conservation of motion. Keep hands close together, a little more than waisthigh.

HOLDING AND TIGHTENING

When the braid gets to be about two inches long, grasp the end between the palm and the second and third fingers of the right hand, with the strands on the right between the thumb and first finger. Grasp the strands on the left between the left thumb and first two fingers, brace the fleshy parts of the thumbs against each other, and, with wrists rigid, force the thumbs apart by moving the elbows toward each other. Fig. 8. This movement will tighten the braid and should be done often enough to keep the edges true and the braid without openings between the strands. For the beginner, it is wise to lay the braid along a table or other straight edge occasionally to see that the edges are being kept true.

SPLICING

For a uniform braid, the strands must be kept an even width; so, when the end of a strand begins to narrow,

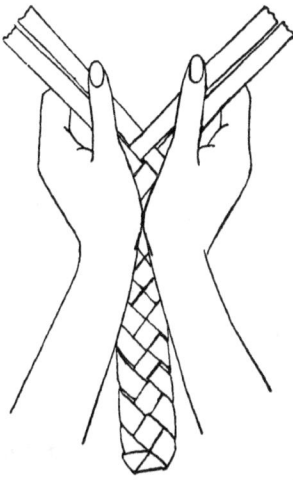 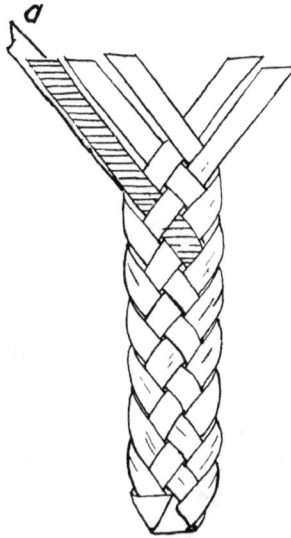 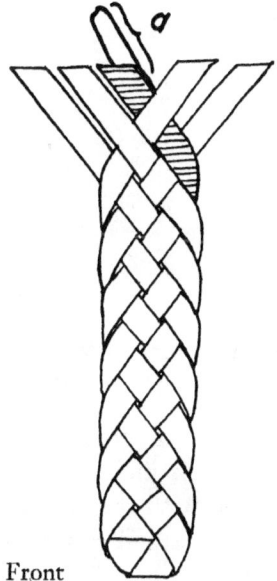

Back   Front

Fig. 8   Fig. 9   Fig. 10

FIGURE 8. Position of hands for holding and tightening braid. FIGURE 9. The back of the braid. Position "a" shows the new strand (which is crosshatched for the sake of clarity) in position immediately behind the old strand, which has become too narrow to hold the braid to the necessary width. FIGURE 10. The braid turned front side up, with position "a" showing the narrow strand with the new strand being woven along with it into the braid. The narrow strand is now ready to be trimmed off, allowing the new strand to be braided just as if it were the old, narrow strand.

take a new strand, cut the end on a slant so that it will fit the edge of the braid, turn the braid over on the back, and slip the new strand, point down, behind the strand to be spliced and into the pocket on the edge of the braid. Fig. 9. Turn the braid front up again and proceed as if the two strands were one until after an edge has been reached and the strands turned over together once. Fig. 10. This turn will prevent the slipping of the new strand.

The old strand should be cut off on the back close to the inside edge of the second or third strand, counting from the outside. It is then fastened securely and, if cut close to a check, is almost invisible.

When a strand needs to be lengthened, allow at least 1½ inches on the old strand in order to provide for the lap and turn on the edge. The splice in crosshatch, Figs. 9 and 10, shows the procedure.

Chapter III

BRAIDS

UNEVEN-NUMBER STRAND CHECK WEAVE

The Beginning: Take a strand about ¼ inch wide and make a V, Fig. 11-*a*, with the left leg under. Lay another strand horizontally in the fold of the V. Fig. 11-*b*. Arrange the strands so that the ends are uneven, as the splicing of the strands must be done one at a time and some inches apart in order to make a strong braid. Holding the two strands together at the fold of the V, take end 4 and fold it flat over end 2, which gives Fig. 11-*c*.

Next fold strand 2 over strand 4 and weave it under strand 1 which makes a double V. Fig. 11-*d*. This is called by old braiders "the button." It is highly necessary that this step be mastered because the "button" is the beginning for so many procedures, and all instructions in which it is used depend on the sequence given. It gives a neat belt beginning, furnishes a starting point for sewed braids, and gives the proper angles of strands in many complex braid procedures.

Take another strand and insert it butt end down under strand 2 where it crosses strand 4. Fig. 11-*e*. Pull through until the strand narrows. Turn the long end of this strand back toward the ends of the strands which make the button, Fig. 11-*f*, and *turn the braid over so that the inserted strand is on the back*. Fig. 11-*g*.

Grasp both ends of the new strand, which is now on the left, and bring them to the top and weave over one and under one. Fig. 11-*h*. This strand is added in this manner in order to anchor it firmly. The tip of it should be carried along under the strand and cut off closely as soon as the braid is well started. The right-hand side of the braid now has three strands, so the outer right strand is folded, face down, and woven over one, under one. Fig. 11-*i*. The left side then has three strands, so the outer strand is folded to the top and woven over one, under one. Fig. 11-*j*. Proceed, working on alternate sides.

EVEN-NUMBER STRAND CHECK WEAVE

Make a button as described in the beginning of this chapter under Uneven-Number Strand Check Weave, Figs. 11-*a-d*, and number the ends of the strands 1, 2, 3, 4, beginning at left side.

24

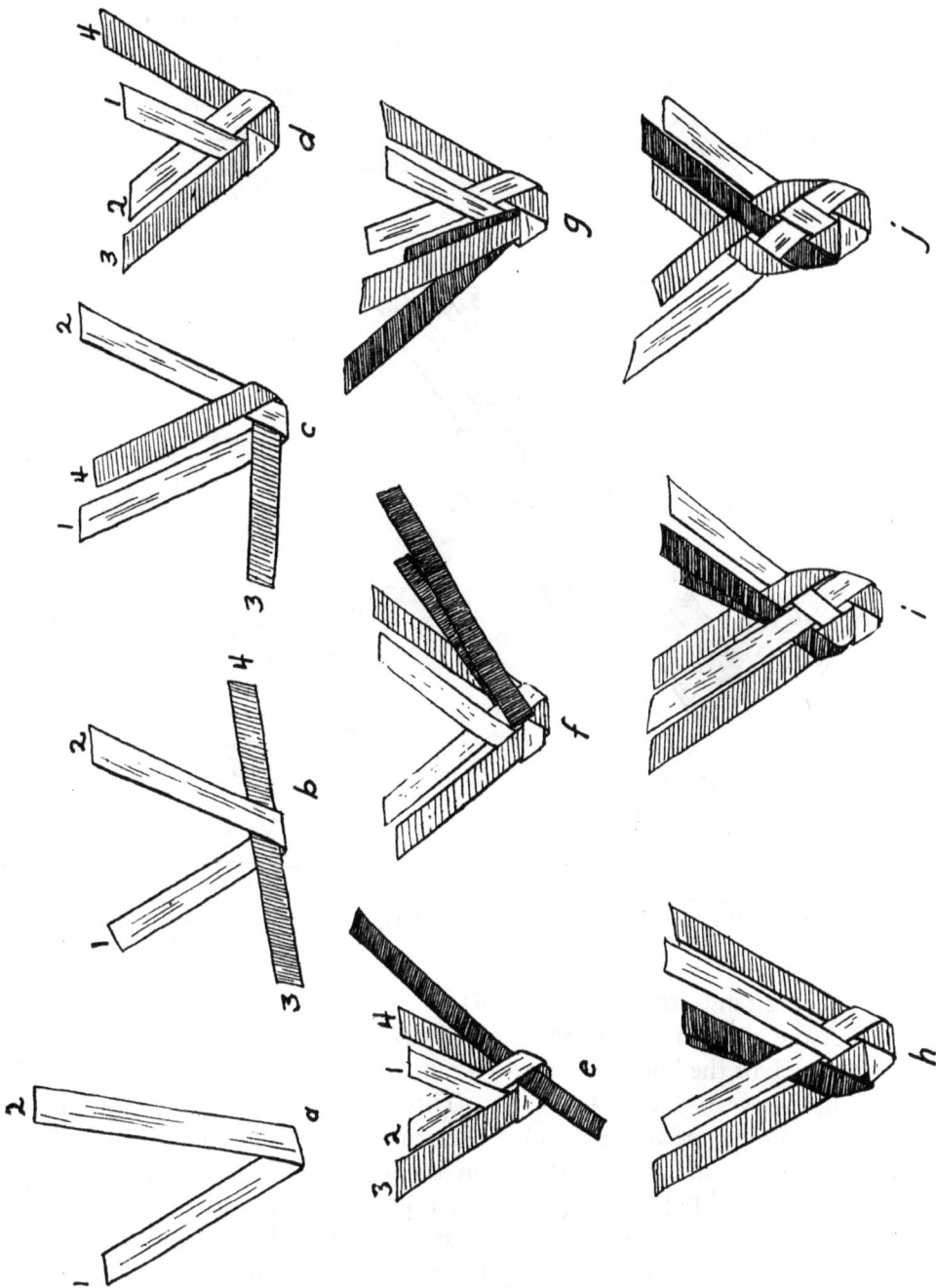

FIGURE 11. UNEVEN-NUMBER STRAND, CHECK WEAVE. Step-by-step procedure.

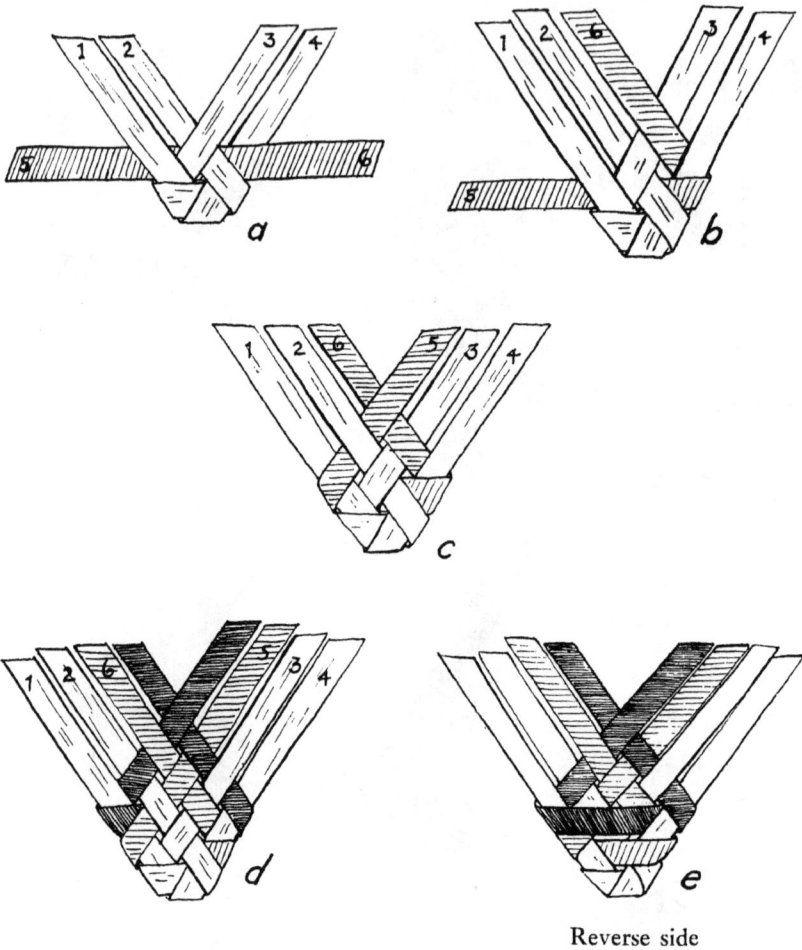

Reverse side

FIGURE 12. Detail of EVEN-NUMBER STRAND, CHECK-WEAVE BRAID.

Lay another strand, the left end numbered 5, the right end numbered 6, across the back of the button. Bring number 6 up between 3 and 4, Fig. 12-a, back down *over* and *under* 4 and up again between 3 and 4, where it parallels 2. Fig. 12-b. Pull left end 5 tight and weave it over 1 and under 2 and over 6. Fig. 12-c. Proceed as instructed in Rule II, as follows:

RULE II. *In all even-number strand braids the edge strands turn one over, one under.*

This beginning provides for the over turn on the left, the under turn on the right, and has six strands. It could just as well be any even number of strands. The rule controls the turning of the edge strands, and the rest of the braid is woven in check weave.

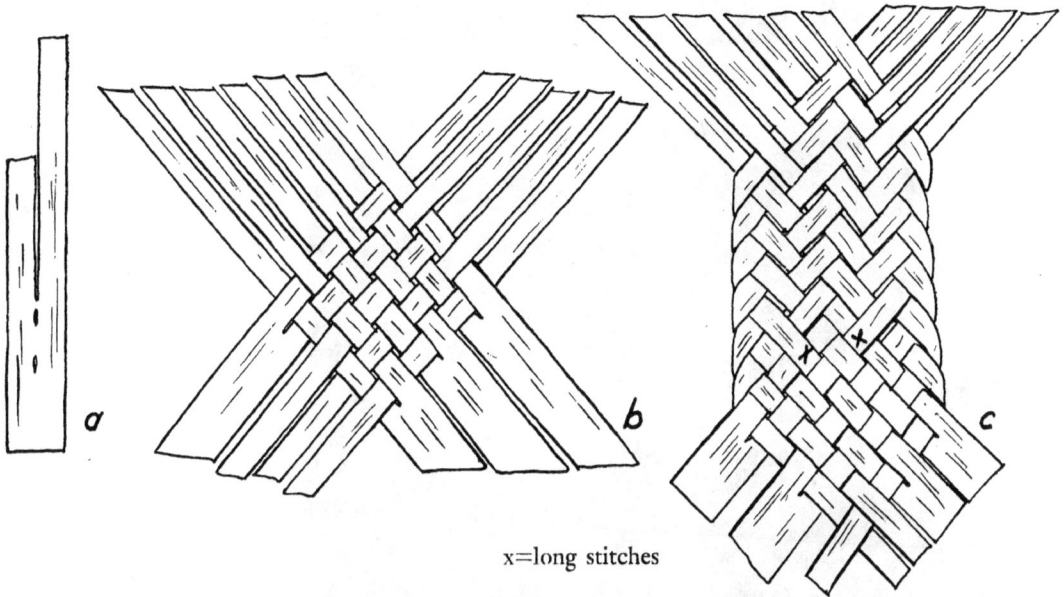

x=long stitches

FIGURE 13. Detail of herringbone weave. *a*. Preparation of frond, leaving one or more weavers fastened together at butt or stem end. *b*. Fronds laced together and position of strands so weaving may be started. *c*. Long stitches in changing from check weave to herringbone and detail of herringbone weave.

* Weave from the right under one, over one, weave from the left over one, under one, over one.* Repeat procedure between stars (*). Weave on alternate sides. Keep braid firm and edges true.

The numbering of the strands is for the beginner only. The routine should be practiced until no help is needed.

If a wider braid with more weavers is desired, they may be added similarly, except that the end of the inserted strands must be brought up on alternate sides—that is, the left end of the next strand would be brought up between 1 and 2, back over and under one, and up again between 1 and 2, and the right end woven over 4, under 3, and over 5, and under the left end of the weaver. Fig. 12-*d*. The reverse side of this is in Fig. 12-*e*.

HERRINGBONE BRAID

Of all the braids, this one gives more for the time and effort expended, as it is easily and quickly made, is decorative, and at the same time sturdy. It is an old favorite. Examples of it may be found in primitive braids, basketry and other crafts, in splint chair bottoms, and in the products of today's craftsmen.

The appearance is greatly altered by the width of the strands as a comparison of the two examples given will show. Fig. 13-*d-e*.

Fig. 13-*d*   Fig. 13-*e*   Example 3.   Fig. 14A   Fig. 15

FIGURE 13-*d*. How long stitches appear in the beginning of finished herringbone weave and how braid should look. *e*. Same braid made of narrow weavers and illustrating that braid can be made of narrow straws or materials to good effect. EXAMPLE 3. Hybrid of herringbone weave due to wrong number of strands in braid composition. FIGURE 14A. Curve-edge braid. FIGURE 15. Curve-edge band.

Rule III. *Herringbone braid can be made only with a number of strands divisible by 4, plus 3. The number of strands usually employed is 7 or 11.*

The interesting hybrid shown in the photograph of a braid marked "Example 3" is the result of a pupil's effort to make a herringbone weave with nine strands.

Another method of starting braids, and the one most frequently used when a finished end is not desired, is given in these examples. Prepare eleven strands ³⁄₁₆ inch wide, but exercise care to leave several of them fastened together at the butt or stem end of the frond. Fig. 13-*a*. These are laced together as shown in Fig. 13-*b*. Note that as this is an uneven-strand braid, the edge strands turn to the top. Arrange so that six strands point left and five strands point right.

* Weave over one, under two, over two from the left. Weave over one, under two, over two from the right.* Repeat procedure between stars (*).

In changing from the check weave (with which the fronds are fastened together) to the herringbone weave, two long stitches, as marked at X on Fig. 13-*c-d*, always show up on the front of the braid. This is their only appearance and, as they are at the end of the braid, they may be allowed for and cut off.

This braid is suitable for the construction of belts, underarm purses, shopping bags, floor mats, seat covers, and other articles. Fig. 16 shows a well-constructed shopping bag.

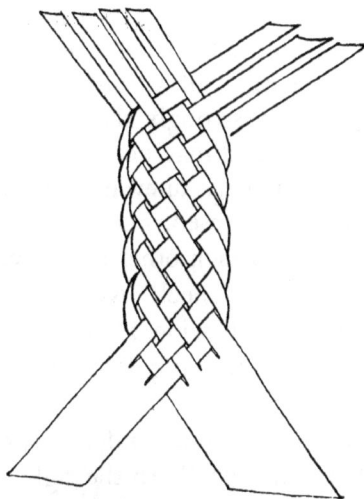

FIGURE 14B. Detail drawing of procedure of curve-edge braid.

A particularly smart book cover can be made by stitching wide braid together vertically, with edges of the narrow herringbone, which will also serve as a finishing braid. Fig. 65-*a-b*.

Hats, too, are a possibility if the braid is made of seven strands or of eleven narrow strands. The wide braid does not lend itself to the necessary curve for millinery.

Splice and tighten as in uneven-strand check weave.

CURVE-EDGE BRAID
(Fig. 14AB)

This is one of the simplest of the fancy-edged braids, is quickly made, and lends itself to a wide variety of articles either for entire construction or as an edge braid. It may be made with an even number of strands, in which case the under turn should be arranged to come on the inner straight edge. However, it will be a most unusual purpose which will not lend itself to the using of an uneven-strand braid which is strongly recommended. Width of strand may be from ⅛ inch to ⁵⁄₁₆ inch. Any uneven number of strands may be used.

Weave into each other at undivided butt ends in check weave, seven strands ³⁄₁₆ inch wide. Divide to have four strands pointing left and three pointing right.

* Weave over one, under one, over one from the left. Turn the right outside strand over so that it is underside up, using an under turn, and weave it over one, under one, over one.* Repeat procedure between stars (*).

Do not crease the turn: it is a curve which can be made more pronounced, and the edge evened by giving it a sharp tug from the right.

Keep braid tight and edges true.

CURVE-EDGE BAND
(Fig. 15, p. 28)

Useful as a trimming band or for putting plain braids together.

Weave into each other at undivided butt ends, check weave, seven strands ⅛ inch wide divided four strands pointing right, three pointing left. * Turn the right outer strand, underside up, using an under turn, and weave over one, under one, over one. Turn the left outer strand underside up, using an under turn, and weave over one, under one, over one.* Repeat procedure between stars (*).

Do not crease turns but make tight

curves by sharp tugs on the ends of the strands. Keep braid tight and edges true.

NOTE: Curve edges are same as illustrated for curve-edge-braid.

CURVE-EDGE VARIATION
(Fig. 17AB, pp. 32, 33)

For use as edge braid or for entire construction.

Weave into each other at undivided butt ends, check weave, eight strands ⅛ inch to ³⁄₁₆ inch wide, divided four strands each pointing right and left and so arranged that the under turn of the even-number strand braid is on the outer or left edge.

* Weave over one, under one, over one from the right. Turn strand 2 on the left underside up, using an under turn, and weave over one, under one, over one. Pull end of strand 2 to tighten curve. Weave over one, under one, over one from the right. Turn strand 1 on the left underside up, using an under turn, and weave under one, over one, under one, over one.* Repeat procedure between stars (*).

Pull strand 1 to make a slight arc over the curve.

Keep braid firm and edges true.

POINT-EDGE BRAID
(Fig. 18, p. 33)

A simple, general-purpose braid, useful for an entire hat or for a decorative edge for the brim only for a hat made of plain braid. Two lengths of it laced together with a thong of palmetto were used to furnish ventilation

FIGURE 16. Shopping bag of eleven-strand, herringbone-weave braid. It takes 12 to 15 yards of braid 1¼ inches to 1½ inches wide to make this bag.

midway of the crown of a man's hat. Three or more lengths of braid so laced together form the sides of an attractive candy basket for Valentine's Day or for Easter.

Weave into each other at undivided butt ends· six strands about one-eighth inch wide divided three strands each pointing right and left. * Weave over one, under one from the right. Weave strand 2 on the left over one, under one. Weave over one, under one from the right. Turn strand 1 on the left, underside up, using an under turn, and weave under one, over one, under one.* Repeat procedure between stars (*).

Adjust the point made by strand 1 to about twice the height of the strand width. This procedure results in a firm, inner, five-strand braid with a pointed edge. The apex of each point is directly above the inner braid turn and the front base of each point crosses the end of the last point between each turn of the inner braid, which is every third check.

Keep inner braid firm, edges true, and points to size.

POINT-EDGE BANDS LACED
(Fig. 19-a-b-c-d)

Another and a more ambitious version of the point edge is given at Fig. 19-a. This is an excellent braid for hats, summer bags, fancy baskets etc. It is a four-strand inner braid with points on both sides made up of bands laced together.

Weave into each other at undivided

FIGURE 17A. Detail of curve-edge-variation braid.

FIGURE 19-a. Point-edge band. b. Point-edge bands laced. Detail of braiding the pattern and lacing together.

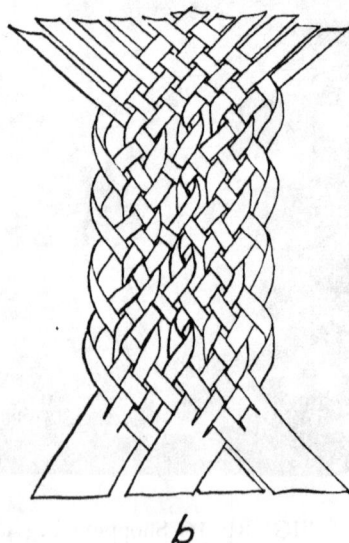

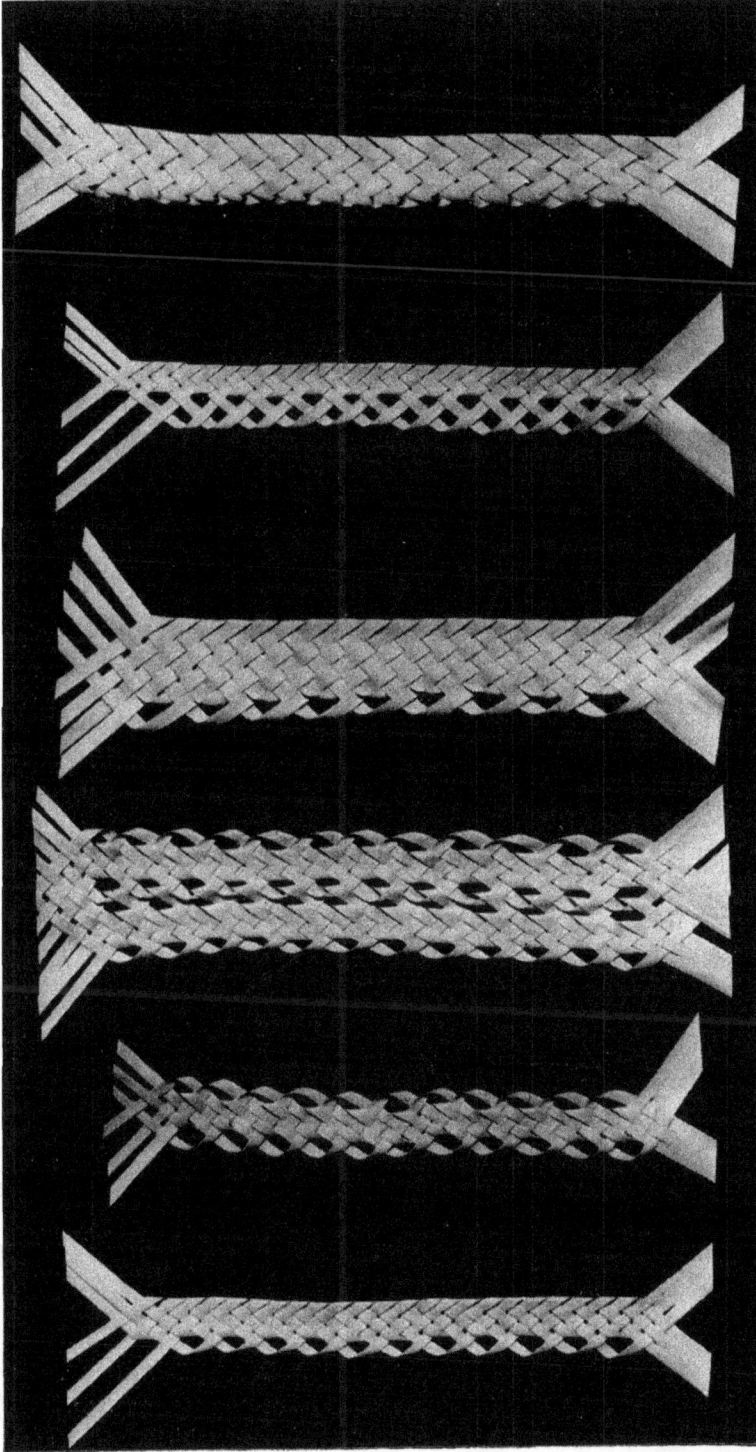

Fig. 18   Fig. 19-*c*   Fig. 19-*d*   Fig. 17B   Fig. 20   Fig. 21

FIGURE 17B. Sample of curve-edge-variation braid. FIGURE 18. Sample of point-edge braid. FIGURE 19-*c*. Sample of point-edge band. FIGURE 19-*d*. Sample of point-edge bands laced. FIGURE 20. Sample of lattice-point-edge braid. FIGURE 21. Sample of hat braid.

33

butt ends, in check weave, six strands ⅛ inch wide. Divide so as to point three strands each right and left. Arrange the weave so that strand 2 on the right turns under for the four-strand core braid.

* Weave strand 2 on the left over one. Weave strand 2 on the right under one, over one. Turn strand 1 on the left, using an under turn, to make a pointed arc. Weave under one, over one. Turn strand 1 on the right, using an under turn, to make a pointed arc, and weave over one, under one, over one.* Repeat procedure between stars (*) until the required length of braid is made.

Start another six-strand braid in the same manner, but, before the pointed arc on the left is turned, slip the strand through the right arc on the first length of braid from the underside, make an under turn, and weave under one, over one. Strand 1 on the right is turned also with an under turn and woven over one, under one, over one. Proceed as in the first length of braid. Note that the beginning of one arc crosses the end of the last one and widens the closely woven part of the braid slightly. These crosses come between the turns which form the inner braid at every third check. A tubular lacing rather than a lock-lace is what the pattern calls for, so care must be exercised to give the under turn to the strands which make the points. The turning of one row of points with an under turn and the interlacing row with an over turn will result in a

closer fitting lock-lace, but not so attractive. Any number of braids may be laced together in the making so as to form the desired width.

If the braid for a basket or a continuous band is wanted, an invisible joining may be made by braiding each row the required length and weaving the ends far enough into each other to make the joint secure, then trimming off ends. Braiding of the second band should be started at such a place on the first braid that the finish of band 2 does not coincide with that of band 1, so strengthening the whole.

LATTICE-POINT EDGE
(Fig. 20, p. 33)

An elaboration of the point edge with a wider decorative edge, unique in its lattice effect. This braid is not as serviceable as the single-point braid, but it is suitable for any service which does not require sturdiness.

Weave into each other at undivided butt ends six strands about ⅛ inch wide in check weave, so arranged that the under turn of the even-strand braid is on the left, and with three strands each pointing right and left.

* Weave over one, under one from the right. Using strand 3 from the left, weave under one. Weave over one, under one from the right.

Turn strand 1 on the left underside up, pass it under strand 2 (which is still unwoven), and weave it into the base braid, over one, under one.

Weave over one, under one from the right. Using the third strand from the left, weave under one. Weave over one, under one from the right.

Turn strand 2 on the left, underside up, pass it under the next lattice strand, and weave it into the base braid, over one, under one.* Repeat procedure between stars (*).

Keep lattice points adjusted evenly, the height approximately four times the width of the strand used or, for an eighth-inch strand braid, one half inch.

The foundation braid is a firm, four-strand braid. For the lattice points, there are always two strands at the top awaiting the proper interval to be woven, which indicates itself as the foundation braid develops.

Note that the beginning of point 3 is crossed by the end of point 1, and the beginning of point 4 is crossed by the end of point 2 at the upper edge of the base braid, widening it slightly. Higher on the points, strand 2 weaves over 1, under 3, and over 4, so producing the lattice.

HAT BRAID
(Fig. 21, p. 33)

This braid may be used for construction of an entire hat or for an edge on a hat made of plain, check-weave braid. This is one of the few fancy-edge braids in which the outer strand is not turned face down or curled in some manner.

Weave into each other at undivided butt ends six strands a scant ¼ inch wide in check weave, 4 pointing right and 2 pointing left, arranging to have under turn on the right. Weave under

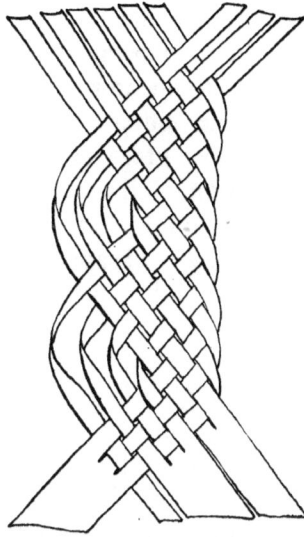

FIGURE 22A. Detail of lace-edge hat braid.

one, over one, under one from the right.

Slip strand 1 on the left, face up, into the weave, over one, under one, pulling to make a firm pointed pucker on the edge. Weave under one, over one, under one from the right. Handle each strand as it comes to the edge in like manner, making a slightly serrated edge.

Decorative and easy.

A variation sometimes seen has every second strand on the left folded under flat as in plain braiding.

LACE-EDGE HAT BRAID
(Fig. 22AB, pp. 35, 37)

This braid, in check weave, is one of the simplest of the fancy-edge braids. A feeling of lightness is desirable, so it should be made slightly loose, which will also help in the necessary curving of the inner edge.

For hat braids, the strands should be narrow. This will make a braid in which the difference in the side of the inner and the outer edges when curved is not so great and so makes the construction of the hat less difficult. A braid should be fairly narrow, also, for the sake of appearance. A heavy, wide braid makes a coarse, clumsy hat.

Nine strands ⅛ inch wide make a nice braid, though a larger or smaller number may be used to taste.

Weave into each other at undivided butt ends nine strands ⅛ inch wide so arranged as to have six strands point left, three strands point right. * Turn under the fourth strand from the left and weave under one, over one. The lower or inner part of this braid is composed of six strands, so the law of the even-number strand braid applies.

Weave over one, under one, over one from the right.

Turn strand 3 on the left, underside up, adjust to make a slight arc and weave over one, under one, over one from the left. Weave over one, under one, over one from the right. Turn strand 2 on the left, underside up, adjust to make a slightly larger arc, and weave under one, over one, under one, over one. Weave over one, under one, over one from the right. Turn strand 1 on the left, underside up, adjust to make an arc slightly larger than that made with strand 2, and weave over one, under one, over one, under one, over one.

Weave over one, under one, over one from the right.*

Repeat procedure between stars (*). Adjust the triple arcs which make up each scallop so they are about the width of the strand distant from each other at their centers. They should be quite close together where the strands enter the inner braid.

Keep inner braid straight and true. All splicing should be done on the straight edge.

LACE-EDGE HAT BRAID WITH BINDING STRAND BETWEEN SCALLOPS
(Fig. 23)

This version of the lace-edge braid gives a firm, less open braid which is achieved very largely by the turning down and weaving into the braid tightly of the strand between the scallops.

There is also the interesting contrast of closely woven and open sections in triangular form.

Weave into each other at undivided butt ends nine strands ³⁄₁₆ inch wide, arranging the strands so as to point six strands to the left and three strands to the right.

* Weave over one from the left with strand 5.

Weave over one, under one, over one from the right. Turn strand 4 on the left underside up, make a slight arc and weave under one, over one.

Weave over one, under one, over one from the right. Turn strand 3 on the left underside up, adjust to make a slightly larger arc, and weave over one, under one, over one.

Weave over one, under one, over one from the right. Turn strand 2 on

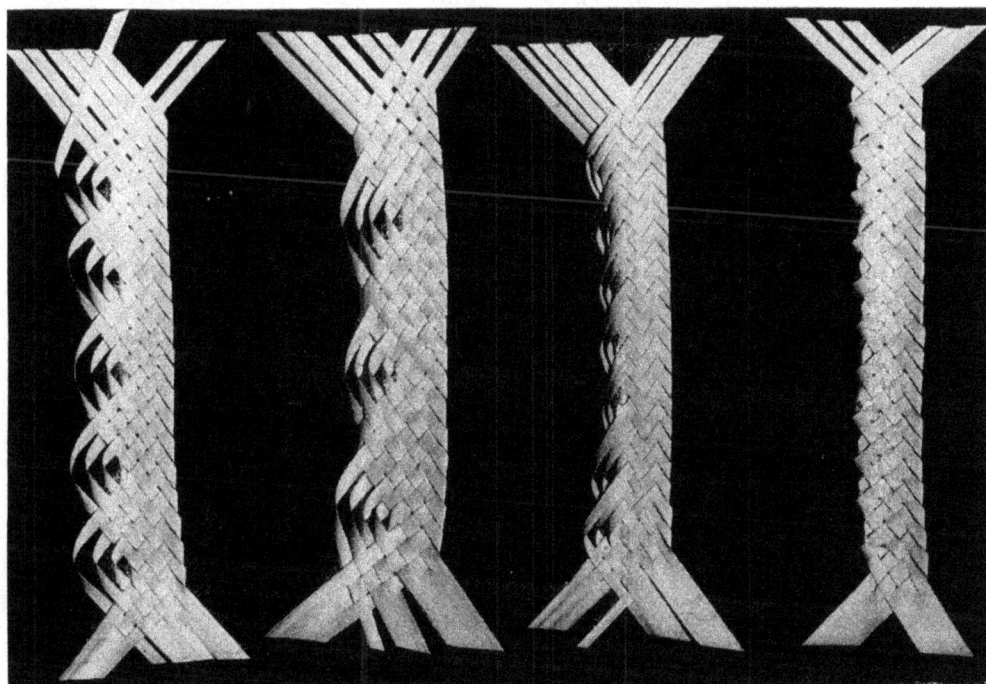

| Fig. 22B. | Fig. 23 | Fig. 24B | Fig. 25 |

FIGURE 22B. Sample of lace-edge hat braid. FIGURE 23. Sample of lace-edge hat braid with binding strand between scallops. FIGURE 24B. Sample of lace braid with overlapping scallops, herringbone base. FIGURE 25. This, the first of the series of braids woven from the back, is the close-curl braid in check weave.

the left underside up, make a slightly longer arc, and weave under one, over one, under one, over one.

Weave over one, under one, over one from the right. Turn strand 1 on the left underside up, form the outer and longer arc of the quadruple-strand scallop and weave over one, under one, over one, under one, over one.

Weave over one, under one, over one, from the right. Fold over the first strand on the left and weave closely over one, under one, over one, under

one, over one. Weave over one, under one, over one from the right.*

Adjust arc strands to make a symmetrical scallop. Strands should be about a strand distant from each other at centers, but closely woven where they leave and enter the braid. Repeat procedure between stars (*).

The braid has a tendency to curve upward. This may be overcome by adjusting scallops correctly and by keeping the inner edge tight and true. Practice will take the beginner over any such problems, as he learns.

37

LACE BRAID WITH OVERLAPPING SCALLOPS, HERRINGBONE BASE

(Fig. 24AB, pp. 37, 38)

A handsome and more unusual form of lace braid is shown in this example. It is a particularly good hat braid, as the construction makes it shape easily.

FIGURE 24A. Detail of lace braid with overlapping scallops, herringbone base.

It also is one of the old favorites but it does not have the circulation it deserves, due, possibly, to the fact that it appears to be intricate. A little study, however, will reveal how very simple it is.

Weave into each other at undivided butt ends ten strands a bare ⅛ inch wide, divided so as to point six strands left, four strands right. The under turn of the even-number strand braid must be on the left.

* Weave over one, under two from the right. With strand 3 on the left, weave closely over two, under two. Weave over one, under two from the right. Turn over strand 2 on the left to make a slight arc and weave over three, under two. Weave over one, under two from the right. Turn over strand 1 on the left to make a slightly larger arc and weave over four, under two.

Weave over one, under two from the right. Adjust triple-strand scallop symmetrically.* Repeat procedure between stars (*).

It will be noted that the front end of each scallop comes on the top, or outside of the scallop, following a procedure not elsewhere used in these instructions. This preserves the herringbone pattern of the inner or base braid, which would not be the case if the scallops were woven into each other, nor would it be possible with ten strands to turn both edge strands to the top as the pattern requires.

If the scallop strands are drawn too tight, the braid will curve up. This must be avoided. Keep inner edge true and herringbone firm.

Chapter IV

BRAIDS WOVEN FROM THE BACK

THE VALUE of this technique lies in the fact that the turns or curls which give the accent to these patterns usually overlay the strands which make them, so it is not only natural that the turn comes first but it is much easier to form the curl on the underside of the braid.

The examples given are so planned as to allow for right-hand manipulation of the pattern, the top or outer edge being at the right. Strand count is from the right.

CLOSE-CURL BRAID IN CHECK WEAVE
(Fig. 25, p. 37)

It will be found that hat braids made with narrow strands give much more satisfactory results. The appearance is daintier and lighter. Also a lightweight, fairly narrow braid adapts itself to the necessary curving in hat construction. See child's bonnet, Fig. 27-a. For some braids, strips ⅛ inch wide are desirable. Others demand a slightly wider strip.

Weave into each other at undivided butt ends six strands ³⁄₁₆ inch wide. As this is an even-strand braid, arrange so the right-hand strand will turn to the top. Divide the strands

evenly, three pointing right and three pointing left.

* Reach under strand 1 on the right to grasp strand 2 with the right thumb and first finger. Turn back and over, windlass fashion, to loop around strand 1, on over itself to provide a seat for the curl, and weave under one. Weave under one, over one, under one from the left.

On the right, turn over strand 1 underside up, and weave over one, under one. Weave under one, over one, under one from the left.* Repeat procedure between stars (*). Do not crease either the curl or the slight arc of the strand over which it is made.

This is an old favorite and has several elaborations, the simplest of which is a single scallop over the curl.

NOTE: For drawing of curl, see Jacksonville braid, Fig. 30A.

CLOSE-CURL BRAID WITH SINGLE-STRAND SCALLOP CHECK WEAVE
(Fig. 26AB, pp. 40, 46)

Weave into each other at undivided butt ends eight strands ³⁄₁₆ inch wide. As this is an even-strand braid, arrange so that the right outer strand

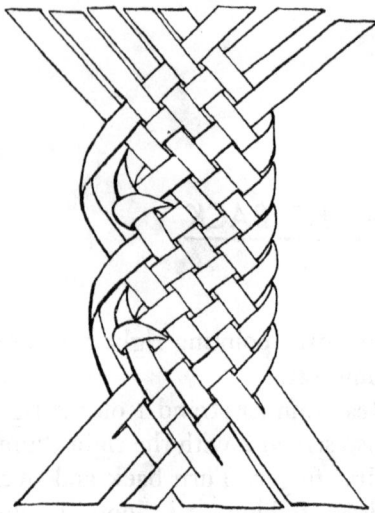
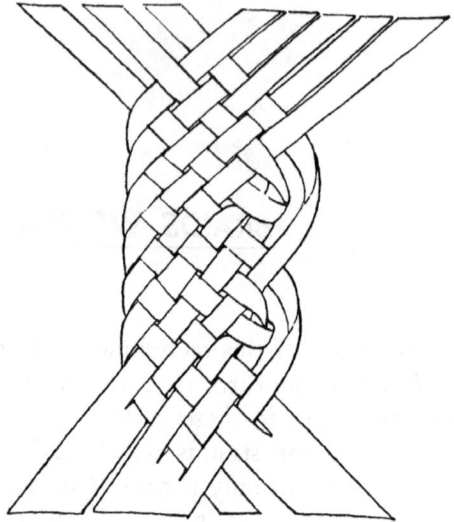

Front   Back

FIGURE 26A. Detail of close-curl braid with single-strand scallop, check weave. The front and back of the braid, as this braid is woven with the back or wrong side facing the braider. The fancy edge or curl is made on the underside, which becomes the front or right side of the braid when sewing the braids together for a finished article. This is one of the first of the "woven-from-the-back" series. If the braider follows directions carefully, no difficulty will be experienced in weaving any of these braids. Figure 26B shows a sample of the right side of the finished braid.

will turn under. This will establish the proper sequence for the third-from-the-right strand, with which the curl is to be made. Divide strands so that five point right and three point left.

* Reach under strands 1 and 2 on the right to grasp strand 3 with the right thumb and first finger. Make a curl on the underside of the braid by turning it, windlass fashion, back and up around strand 2, on over itself so as to form a seat for the curl, and weave under one, over one.

Weave over one, under one, over one from the left. Turn strand 2, the supporting strand, over and weave over one, under one, over one.

Weave over one, under one, over one, from the left. Turn strand 1 on the right, underside up, and weave under one, over one, under one, over one, adjusting to make a symmetrical scallop.

Weave over one, under one, over one, from the left.* Repeat procedure between stars (*).

CLOSE-CURL BRAID WITH TRIPLE-STRAND SCALLOP CHECK WEAVE
(Fig. 28, p. 46)

Weave into each other at undivided butt ends ten strands $3/16$ inch wide. As this is an even-strand braid, arrange so that the under turn is on the

FIGURE 27-*a*. Child's bonnet in natural-color, close-curl braid in check weave and bound with red grosgrain ribbon. Bonnet is tied at the bottom of the back of the crown and the front is tied under the chin. By untying the ribbon at the back of the crown, the bonnet can be packed flat. *b*. Halo hat in natural-color, "Jacksonville braid" (close-curl braid in herringbone weave), with colored, grosgrain ribbon, crown band. Instructions for sewing given in discussion of sewing braids.

right. This will establish the proper sequence of the fifth-from-the-right strand with which the curl is to be made. Divide so that seven strands point right and three strands point left.

* Reach under strands 1, 2, 3, and 4 on the right to grasp strand 5 with the right thumb and first finger. Make a curl on the underside of the braid by turning it, windlass fashion, back and up around strand 4, on over itself to form a seat for the curl, and weave under one, over one. Weave over one, under one, over one, on the left. Turn strand 4 on the right, the supporting strand, underside up, and weave over one, under one, over one.

Weave over one, under one, over one, from the left. Turn strand 3 on the right, underside up, to make an arc, and weave under one, over one, under one, over one.

Weave over one, under one, over one from the left. Turn strand 2 on the right, underside up, and weave over one, under one, over one, under one, over one.

41

Weave over one, under one, over one, from the left. Turn strand 1 and weave under one, over one, under one, over one, under one, over one, adjusting scallop strands symmetrically.

Weave over one, under one, over one, from the left.* Repeat procedure between stars (*).

HAT BRAID WITH GRADUATED CURL SCALLOP CHECK WEAVE
(Fig. 29, p. 46)

This is one of the oldest of the hat braids and gives an elaborate effect with a minimum effort.

Weave into each other at undivided butt ends seven strands a full ⅛ inch wide. Divide so four strands point right, three strands point left.

* Reach under strand 1 to grasp strand 2 with the right thumb and first finger. Make a curl on the underside by turning it, windlass fashion, back and up around strand 1 on over itself to make a seat for the curl, and weave under one, over one. Weave over one, under one, over one, from the left.

Make another curl, slightly longer than the first by turning strand 3, windlass fashion, back and up around strand 1, on over itself to make a seat for the curl, and weave under one, over one. Weave over one, under one, over one, from the left.

Make a third curl, still slightly longer, with strand 4 by turning it, windlass fashion, back and up around strand 1, on over itself to form a seat for the curl, and weave under one,

over one. Weave over one, under one, over one from the left. Turn strand 1 on the right over and weave over one, under one, over one.

Weave over one, under one, over one from the left.* Repeat procedure between stars (*).

Each curl is slightly longer than the last, and strand 1 should be adjusted to support them nicely. For detail drawing of curls, see Fig. 31A.

VARIATION: A wider braid with more strands and more curls per scallop.

CLOSE-CURL BRAID IN HERRINGBONE WEAVE—"JACKSONVILLE BRAID"
(Fig. 30AB, pp. 43, 46)

An old, much-used braid. Featured by a palmetto millinery manufacturer of Jacksonville, Florida, in the seventies as a man's hat braid. Good where any sturdy, decorative braid is wanted. See halo hat in Fig. 27-b.

Weave into each other at undivided butt ends, check weave, seven strands ⅛ inch wide, arranged four strands pointing right, three strands pointing left. Weave over one, under two, from both right and left, to establish the herringbone pattern.

* Reach under strand 1 on the right to grasp strand 2 with the right thumb and first finger. Make a curl on the underside of the braid by turning it, windlass fashion, back and up around strand 1, on over itself to make a seat for the curl, and weave under two.

Weave over one, under two from the left. Turn strand 1 on the right over and weave over one, under two.

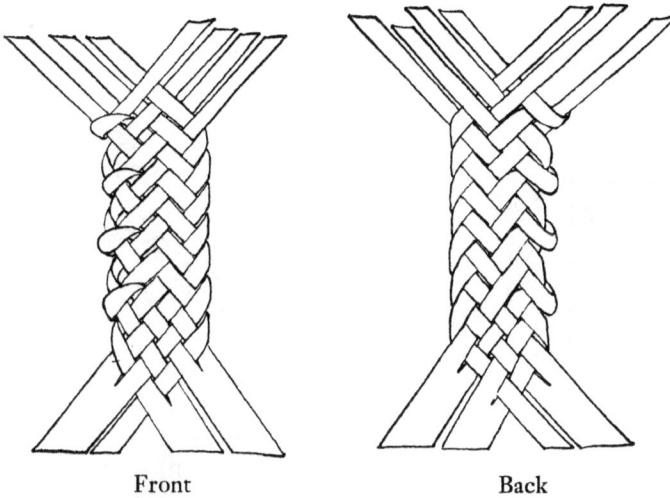

Front   Back

FIGURE 30A. Detail of close-curl braid in herringbone weave—called "Jacksonville braid" because it was the main braid used in the manufacture of hats in factories located in Jacksonville, Florida, during the late 1800's. This is woven from the back, and drawings of both back and front are given to show as much detail as possible. The braider does not see the finished curl until the braid is turned over.

Weave over one, under two from the left.* Repeat procedure between stars (*).

The difference in this example and the first braid of this group is in the basic weave and the number of strands. The long stitch, which always follows a shift from check to herringbone weave, should not be allowed to confuse the braider in getting the work under way. It appears once in this braid and that only at the very beginning.

GRADUATED-CURL SCALLOP, HERRING-BONE WEAVE
(Fig. 31AB, pp. 44, 46)

Weave into each other at undivided butt ends seven strands ⅛ inch wide. Arrange so as to have four strands point right, three strands point left. Weave over one, under two from both right and left to establish the herringbone pattern. No alarm should be occasioned by the one long stitch which will show up in the change from check to herringbone weave.

* Reach under strand 1 to grasp strand 2 with the right thumb and first finger. Make a curl on the underside of the braid by turning it windlass fashion, back and up around strand 1, on over itself to make a seat for the curl, and weave under two. Weave over one, under two from the left.

With strand 3 make another slightly longer curl by turning it back, windlass fashion, up around strand 1, on over itself to make a seat for the

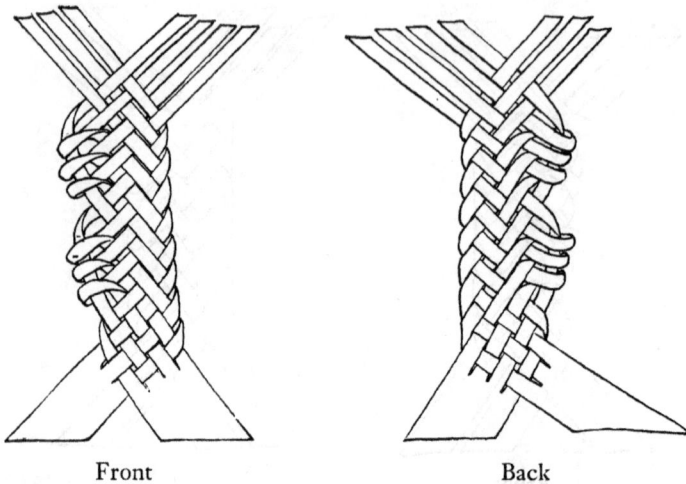

Front   Back

FIGURE 31A. Graduated-curl scallop, herringbone base. A braid woven from the back. Drawing shows both front and back. An easy braid to make and most attractive. As the weavers are narrow, this braid lends itself to a variety of materials. Note the oat-straw braid, Figure 4-a, and the gamma-grass braid, Figure 4-c.

curl, and weave under two. Weave over one, under two from the left.

Make a third, slightly longer curl with strand 4 by turning it, windlass fashion, back and up around strand 1, on over itself to make a seat for the curl, and weave under two. Weave over one, under two from the left. Turn strand 1 on the right over and weave over one, under two. Weave over one, under two from the left.* Repeat procedure between stars (*).

Adjust curls and supporting strand to form a gently ascending scallop.

A BAHAMA ORIGINAL
(Fig. 32AB, pp. 45, 46)

Through attic rummaging, this treasure was discovered in a child's hat made more than twenty-five years ago by the Bahamian servant of a South Florida friend.

Beautifully braided and shaped, the hat proper is made of point-edge braid and finished with three rows of this braid sewed right-side down. This results in an interesting pattern on the upper brim, and puts the curl of the made-from-the-back braid on the under brim, showing in the last row only.

As daintiness is vital to the success of this braid, it should never be attempted with a wide strand.

Weave into each other at undivided butt ends, check weave, ten strands a scant ⅛ inch wide, so arranged that six strands point right and four strands point left and so the under turn of the even-number-strand braid is on the right.

* Weave over one, under two from the left. With strand 4, counting from the right, weave over one, under two. Weave over one, under two from the

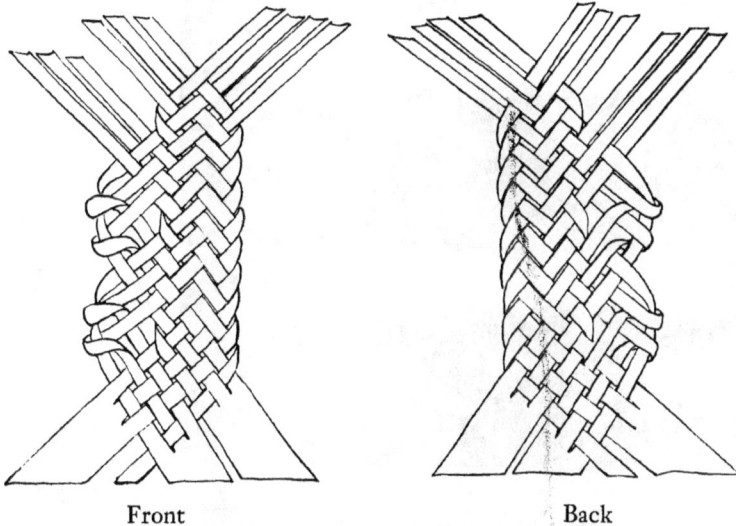

Front   Back

FIGURE 32A. Detail of the Bahama Original braid, woven from the back. The drawings give both front and back detail.

left. Reach under strand 1 on the right, grasp strand 2 and turn it, windlass fashion, up over strand 1, so forming a seat for the curl, and weave under two, over one, under two.

Weave over one, under two from the left. Reach under strand one, grasp strand 3, and make a second curl on the right. Bring the strand up over strand 1 and weave under two, over one, under two.

Weave over one, under two from the left. Turn strand 1 on the right over close to the last curl and weave over one, under two, over one, under two. Tighten braid well.* Repeat procedure between stars (*).

The usual long stitch occasioned by the change of check weave to herringbone weave will be noticed near the beginning on the left. This and the fact that strand 2 comes from under the adjacent strand pointing left, instead of over it, as will be the case in the rest of the braid, should cause no concern. These flaws do not occur after the pattern is set.

The weave should be firm and close in the plain, inner braid. That of the outer edge is controlled largely by the angle of strand 1. A convenient gauge of performance is in the tiny triangle made by the turning to the left of strand 4. This triangle lies immediately below the apex of the scallop and should be equilateral. For best results, splicing must be done in the plain, inner edge.

TWIN CURLS WITH SINGLE-STRAND SCALLOP, HERRINGBONE WEAVE
(Fig. 33AB, pp. 47, 48)

This is a good hat braid, as the construction is such that it lends itself

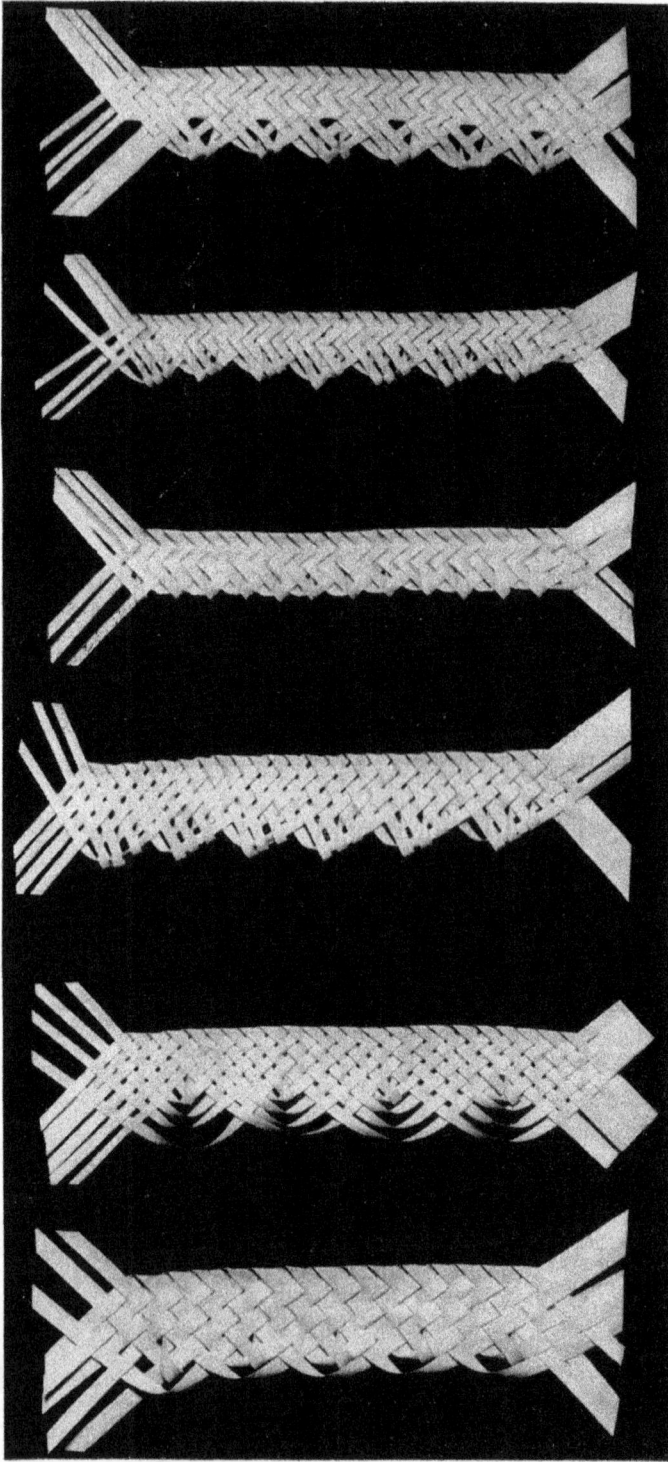

Fig. 26B   Fig. 28   Fig. 29   Fig. 30B   Fig. 31B   Fig. 32B

FIGURE 26B. Sample of close-curl braid with single-strand scallop, check weave. This is woven from the back. FIGURE 28. Sample of close-curl braid with triple-strand scallop, check weave. The detail of the close curl and of the scallop arrangement can be seen in the drawing, Figure 26A. FIGURE 29. Sample of hat braid with graduated-curl scallop, check weave. Detail of the graduated-curl scallop, Figure 31A. The curl is the same, only the base braid being different. FIGURE 30B. Sample of close-curl braid in herringbone weave, "Jacksonville braid." FIGURE 31B. Sample of graduated-curl scallop, herringbone weave.
FIGURE 32B. Sample of a Bahama Original braid.

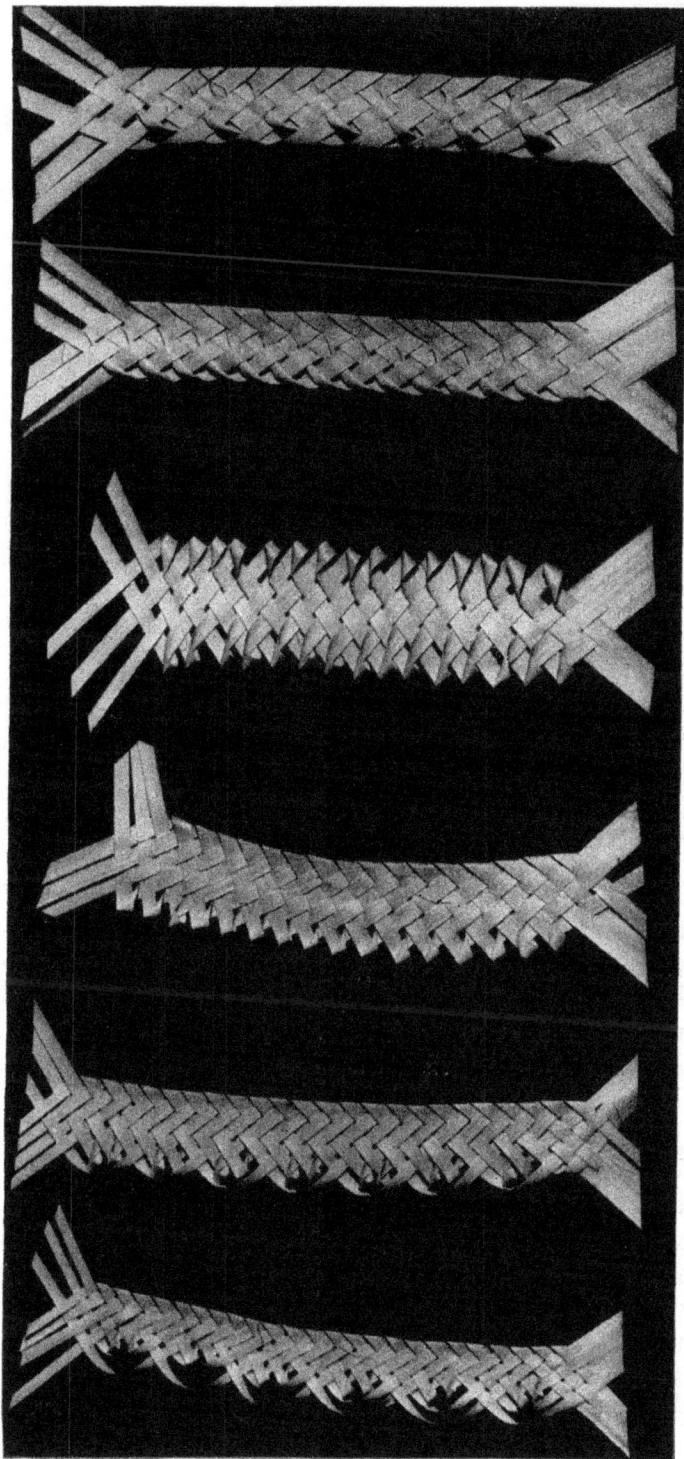

Fig. 34   Fig. 33B   Fig. 35B   Fig. 36   Fig. 37B   Fig. 38

FIGURE 33B. Sample of twin-curl braid with single-strand scallop, herringbone weave. FIGURE 34. Sample of twin curls with double-strand scallop, combination weave. Braid is woven from the back. FIGURE 35B. Sample of close-curl edge without supporting strand. FIGURE 36. Sample of close-curl band without supporting strand. Braid woven from the back. See Figure 35A for detail of curl. FIGURE 37B. Sample of double-shuffle braid. Good finger exercise for occupational therapy. Braid is woven from the back. FIGURE 38. Sample of double-shuffle with single-strand scallop. Braid woven from the back. For detail of triangular pattern fold, see Figure 37A.

47

Front

FIGURE 33A. Detail drawing of front of twin-curl braid with single-strand scallop, herringbone weave. Braid is woven from the back.

particularly well to the necessary shaping.

Weave together at undivided butt ends seven strands a bare 3/16 inch wide. Divide so as to have four strands point left, three strands point right. Weave over one, under two from the left.

* With strand 2 on the right, make an unsupported curl by turning it windlass fashion back and up over to the left to provide a seat for the curl, and weave under two. Weave over one, under two from the left.

Make another curl in the same manner with strand 3 and weave under two. Weave from the left over one, under two. Take up strand 1, on the right, turn it over to make a scallop

over both curls, and weave over one, under two. Weave over one, under two from the left.* Repeat procedure between stars (*).

Keep curls tight, inner edges straight, and scallops even.

TWIN CURLS WITH DOUBLE-STRAND SCALLOP, COMBINATION WEAVE
(Fig. 34, p. 47)

The neat little pattern of checks at the base of the scallops and the single pairs of herringbone stitches are the unusual features of this interesting hat braid. Though it is one of the old patterns, it is not often seen.

Weave into each other at undivided butt ends seven strands 1/8 inch wide. Divide so as to have four strands point right, three strands point left.

* Leave strands 1 and 2 free at the right edge and make an unsupported curl on the underside of the braid with strand 3 by turning it, windlass fashion, back, up, and over to the left to make a seat for the curl. Weave under one. Weave from the left over one, under two.

Make another curl with strand 4 in the same manner and weave under one. Weave from the left over one, under two.

Take up strand 2 on the right, turn it over to make the inner scallop over the curls and weave it into the braid over one, under one.

Weave from the left over one, under two. Turn strand 1 on the right over to make the outer scallop and weave under one, over one, under one. Weave from the left over one,

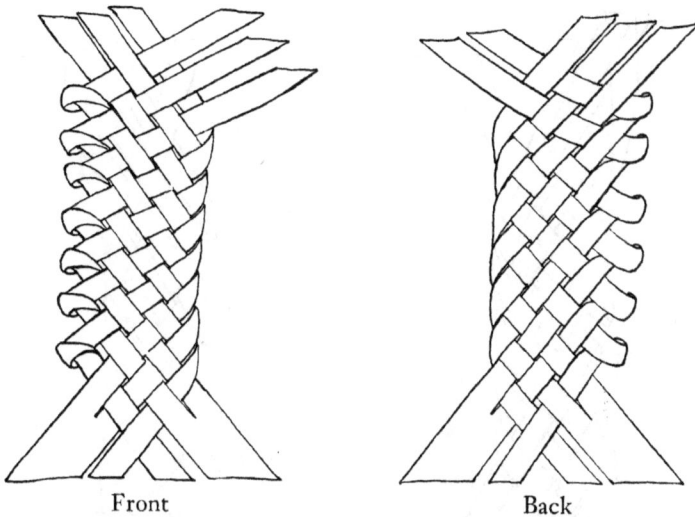

Front   Back

FIGURE 35A. Detail drawing of front and back of close-curl edge braid without supporting strand. Braid woven from the back.

under two.* This is the complete motif. Repeat procedure between stars
(*). Detail of curls and scallops same
as Fig. 33A.

Keep curls tight, inner edge firm
and scallops even.

CLOSE-CURL EDGE WITHOUT
SUPPORTING STRAND
(Fig. 35AB, pp. 47, 49)

This example is of particular value
for edging on round or oval surfaces,
as, having no controlling outer-edge
strand, it accommodates itself nicely
to curving. This, also, is another of
that large group of braids woven from
the back.

Weave into each other at undivided
butt ends six strands $\frac{3}{16}$ inch wide, so
arranged that the under turn of the
even-number-strand braid is on the
right and with three strands pointing
each right and left.

* Weave over one, under one from
the left. Grasp strand 1 on the right
and make a complete turn, forming a
curl on the underside, and weave under one, over one, under one.* Repeat procedure stars (*).

The width must be kept accurately
gauged, which is not quite as easily
done as when the pattern calls for a
supporting strand for the curl. If the
braid curves to the inner side while in
the making, so much the better. Splicing should be made on the inner, plain
side.

CLOSE-CURL BAND WITHOUT
SUPPORTING STRAND
(Fig. 36, p. 47)

This example is similar to the preceding braid but much less practical.
As the band does not have the inner
straight edge for a stabilizer, it is

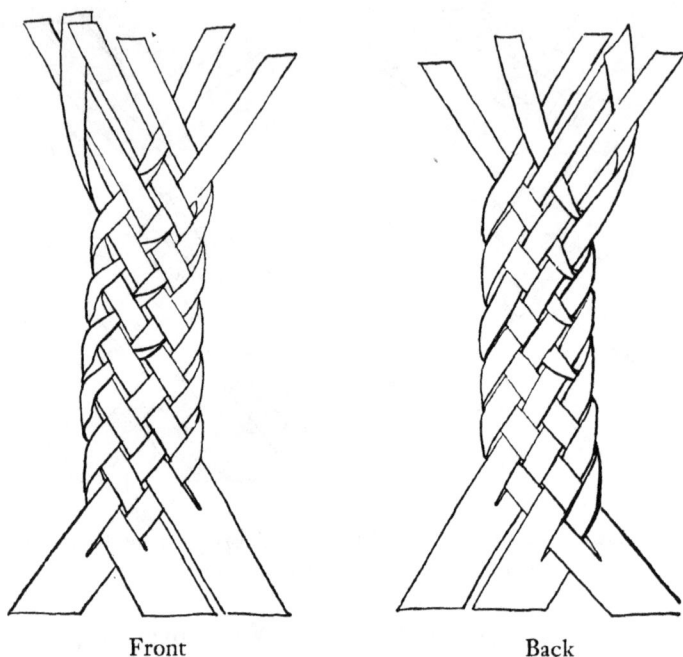

Front   Back

FIGURE 37A. Detail drawing of front and back of double-shuffle braid.

much less sturdy. Too, edges are much more usable than bands.

Weave into each other at undivided butt ends five strands ¼ inch wide, divided so as to point three strands right, two strands left.

* Grasp strand 1 on the right, make a complete turn to form an unsupported curl on the underside of the braid, and weave over one, under one.

Grasp strand 1 on the left, make a complete turn to form an unsupported curl on the underside of the braid and weave over one, under one.* Repeat procedure between stars (*). Right and left curls are identical, but unless the braider has unusual dexterity, the left curls will be much more difficult.

Detail of curl may be seen in Fig. 35A.

DOUBLE-SHUFFLE
(Fig. 37AB, pp. 47, 50)

The method of making the pattern accent for this braid and for the double-shuffle with single scallop—though they, too, are woven from the back—is a distinctly different procedure from that of the curl series.

This example is a particularly good finger exercise, but it has little to recommend it otherwise, except for the sake of variety and of basic procedure involved.

Weave into each other at undivided butt ends six strands ³⁄₁₆ inch wide, divided so as to have four strands point right, two strands point left. Arrange the under turn of the even-number-strand braid for the right.

Weave under one, over one, under one from right. Weave over one, under one from left.

* Grasp strand 1 on the right and give it an under turn as if preparing to weave it under strand 2, but, before weaving, give it another half turn, which will make a complete rotation of the strand and so form an elongated triangular fold. Weave under one, over one, under one. Weave over one, under one, from the left.* Repeat procedure between stars (*).

For best results work almost dry material.

DOUBLE-SHUFFLE WITH SINGLE-STRAND SCALLOP
(Fig. 38, p. 47)

Weave into each other at undivided butt ends six strands three-sixteenths inch wide. Divide to point four strands to the right, two to the left. Arrange for the under turn of the even-number-strand braid to be on the left. Use almost dry material.

Weave over one, under one, over one from right. Weave under one, over one from left.

* Turn strand 2 on the right as if preparing to weave it under strand 3, but, before weaving it, finish the turn so that the strand has been given a complete rotation, so producing the triangular pattern fold. Weave under one, over one.

Weave under one, over one from the left. Turn strand 1 on the right to make a close-fitting scallop over the pattern fold, and weave over one, under one, over one.

Weave under one, over one from the left.* Repeat procedure between stars (*). An unusual, sturdy braid.

Chapter V

THE SPIRALS

(Woven from the Back)

In the braid examples previously given, the pattern accents have been accomplished by manipulations of one or more of the strands and largely by use of points, scallops, or close curls.

Examination of the braids in this group will show a different kind of curl, one made by a complete turn of the strand. If difficulty is found in establishing the routine, a mark about an inch long up the face of the strand on the underside (for braids in this group, too, are woven from the back) will be helpful.

The spiral, like the close curl, is made over a supporting strand, which also serves to give space between spirals in the greater part of the patterns. The close curl is made largely with an arm movement; the spirals are formed with a wrist movement which helps make the tightly curled tip.

The braids in this group are not seen frequently, nor are they indispensable; however, no discussion of braids which disregards them is complete.

SIMPLE SPIRAL, CHECK WEAVE
(Fig. 39AB, pp. 53, 54)

Weave into each other at undivided butt ends six strands $\frac{3}{16}$ inch wide so arranged as to have the under turn of the even-number-strand braid on the left. Divide to have three strands point right, three strands point left.

* Weave under one, over one from the left. Reach under strand 1 on the right, grasp strand 2 close to the weave with the first finger and thumb, and, using a quick, upward, wrist movement, turn stand 2 entirely over, being sure that the tip of the spiral is sharply pointed. Fold loosely over strand 1 and weave under one, over one. As in the close-curl series, the strand forms a seat for its spiral.

Weave under one, over one from the left. Turn strand 1, and weave over one, under one, over one from the right.* Repeat procedure between stars (*).

The slight uncreased arc of strand 1, and the loose, straight fold of the spiral strand over it, make up an interesting pattern. Firm, serviceable.

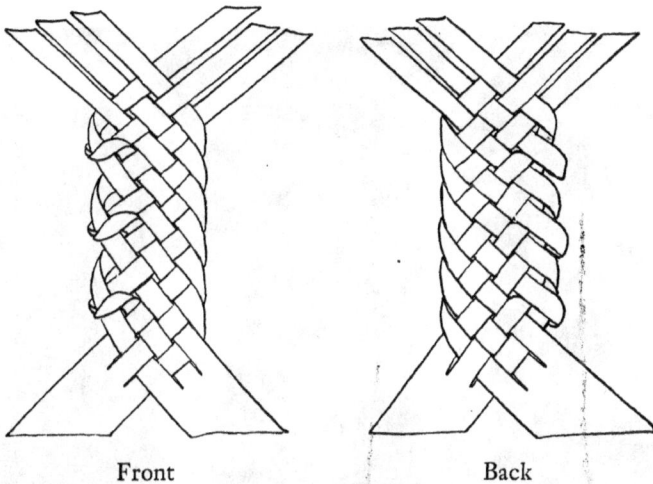

Front　　　　　　　Back

FIGURE 39A. Simple spiral braid, check weave, woven from the back. Detail shows both back and front of braid. A splendid wrist-movement exercise for use in occupational therapy.

SHOOTING STAR AND SPIRAL EDGE
(Figs. 40AB, 41, pp. 54, 55)

The two following braids give an excellent example of the great change in appearance a small change in procedure can make. The basic weaves, of course, are different and the number of strands is not the same, but the spirals are identical in construction.

Interesting though ornate.

Shooting Star, Check-Weave Base

Weave into each other at undivided butt ends six strands $3/16$ inch wide, so arranged as to have the under turn of the even-number-strand braid on the left. Divide to have four strands point right, two strands point left.

* Make two complete forward turns with strand 1 and weave over one, under one, over one. The first of these turns should be very tight so that it will stand erect and about one-half

inch long. The motif might be a pennant with the staff which carries it. Some ease, therefore, is desirable in the strand after the last turn is made. Weave under one, over one from the left. Weave over one, under one, over one from the right. Weave under one, over one, from the left.* Repeat procedure between stars (*).

Useful as an edge braid. Fig. 40AB.

Spiral-Edge Braid, Herringbone Base

Weave into each other at undivided butt ends seven strands $1/8$ inch wide divided so as to point four strands right and three left. Weave over one, under two from both right and left twice, to establish the herringbone pattern.

* Reach under strand 1 on the right, grasp strand 2, and make two complete forward turns, using the upward, wrist-and-hand movement. Fold

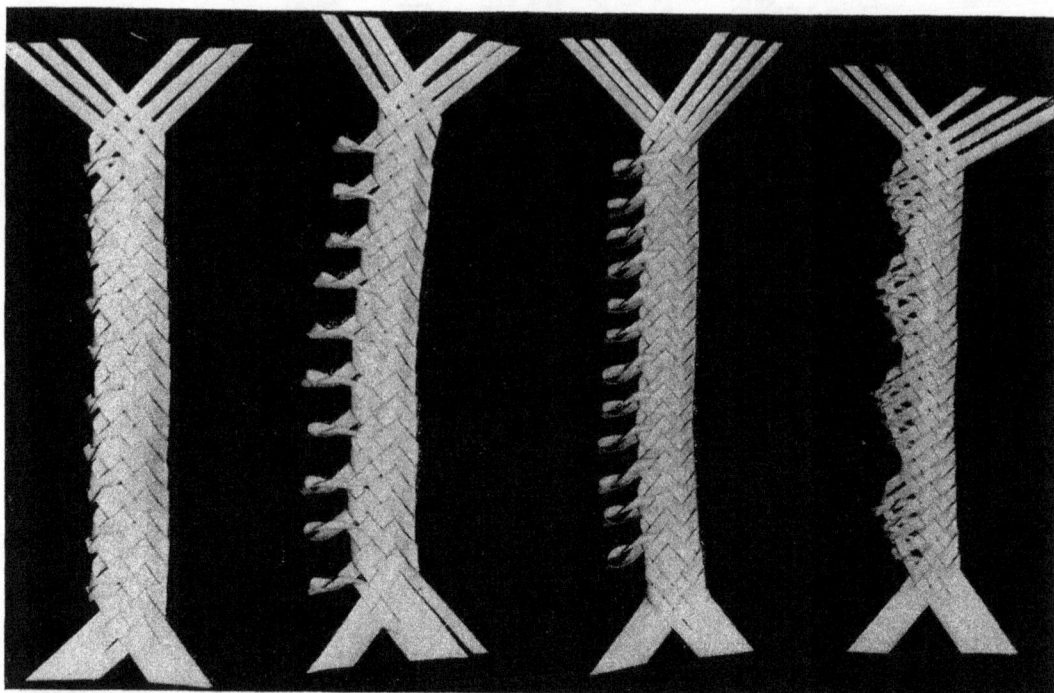

| Fig. 39B | Fig. 40B | Fig. 41 | Fig. 42B |

FIGURE 39B. Sample of the simple spiral braid, check weave. FIGURE 40B. Sample of the shooting-star braid, check-weave base. FIGURE 41. Sample of spiral-edge braid, herringbone base. Detail of spiral may be seen in Figure 40A. FIGURE 42B. Sample of graduated scallop of double-turned spirals, check weave.

loosely over strand 1 to make a spiral about ½ inch long, and weave under two.

Weave over one, under two from the left. With strand 1, weave over one, under two from the right.

Weave over one, under two from the left.* Repeat procedure between stars (*).

In contrast to the spiral in the other braid of this pair, this spiral is made very loose, stands at an angle, and the strand with which it is made is woven back on itself to provide it with a seat. Useful as an edge braid. Fig. 41.

GRADUATED SCALLOP OF DOUBLE-TURNED SPIRALS, CHECK WEAVE
(Fig. 42AB)

One of the myriad small shells of the tropical beaches might well have been the inspiration for this braid. It was a rare find for us, for the usual braider did not know it. The binding strand between scallops serves to make firmer its tight, even weave. It is essentially a dainty braid and should not be attempted with a wide strand.

Weave into each other at undivided butt ends seven strands a scant ⅛ inch

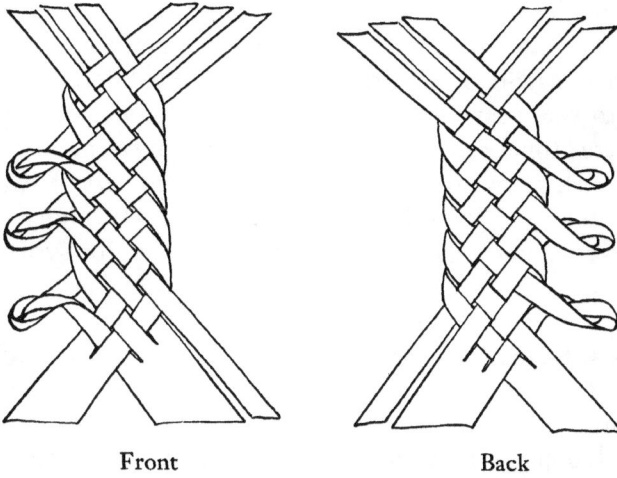

Front   Back

FIGURE 40A. Detail drawing of front and back, shooting-star braid.

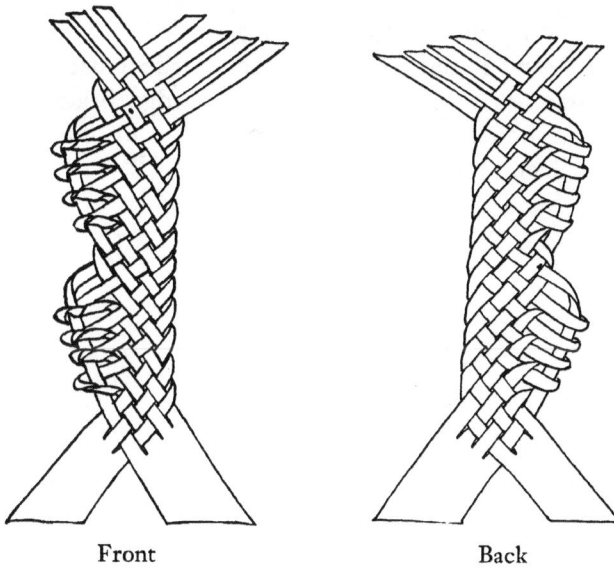

Front   Back

FIGURE 42A. Graduated scallop of double-turned spirals, check weave. An unusual braid. Spirals look like tiny seashells. Braid is woven from the back.

wide. Divide to have four strands point right, three left.

* Reach under strand 1 to grasp strand 2 close to the weave, and give it two complete forward turns to form a double-turn spiral, being sure to make a tight tip. Fold loosely over strand 1, and weave under one, over one.

Weave over one, under one, over one from the left. Reach under strand 1, grasp strand 3, and form a second double-turn spiral, slightly larger than the first. Fold loosely over strand 1 and weave under one, over one.

Weave over one, under one, over one from the left. Reach under strand 1, grasp strand 4, and form the third double-turn spiral, still a little larger. Fold loosely over strand 1, and weave under one, over one.

Weave over one, under one, over one from the left. Reach under strand 1, grasp strand 5, with which the final and longest of the double turn spirals is made. Fold loosely over strand 1, and weave under one, over one.

Weave over one, under one, over one from the left. Turn strand 1 and weave over one, under one, over one. Adjust scallop for symmetry.

Weave over one, under one, over one from the left. Weave in the binding strand from the right, over one, under one, over one. Tighten. Weave over one, under one, over one from the left.* Repeat procedure between stars (*).

The individual scallops will almost adjust themselves if strand 1 is allowed to stand at its angle while they are being made.

An excellent hat braid either alone or as an edge braid of two or three rows only, in combination with a plainer braid.

Chapter VI

FANCY BRAIDS

THE FOLLOWING braids of unusual pattern are sturdy, easily woven and lend themselves to the making of many beautiful and useful articles.

OPEN WEAVE HAT BRAID
(Fig. 43, p. 61)

For an unusually attractive hat, sturdy, yet light in weight, a braid of fifteen strands, $\frac{1}{16}$ inch wide, loosely woven so as to leave space of about $\frac{1}{16}$ inch between strands, is ideal. See Fig. 44, p. 58. For trimming band, see Fig. 55, p. 71.

Any number of strands may be used, but fifteen was chosen because it is an uneven number, consequently the easiest to braid, and the finished product is a good hat-braid width, about $1\frac{1}{4}$ inches.

Rule 1 in Chapter II covers the procedure. If desired, the brim might be finished with any finely woven fancy edge.

COMBINATION-WEAVE HAT BRAID
(Fig. 45, p. 61)

This, an open, lacy weave with its perforation and the lace stripe, makes a most attractive and unusual braid, also light in weight. The development of the pattern necessitates quite a wide braid, and though this is a handicap in hatmaking, it contributes to lightness. Too, the construction is such that it lends itself nicely to shaping. See Fig. 46, p. 59.

It is the most intricate braid of all those given, employing, as it does, both herringbone and check weaves, with the additional hurdles of perforation, lace stripe, even-edge-top scallop, and an up-and-down movement with the same weaver. It is, nevertheless, easy to master even by a braider of limited experience who will follow instructions exactly.

Weave into each other at undivided butt ends eleven strands $\frac{1}{8}$ inch wide, divided so as to point four strands to the right, seven to the left.

* Weave over one, under two from the right. With strand 5 (counting from the left) weave over one, under two, to make the first of the two folds for the bottom of the perforation.

Weave over one, under two from the right. Finish the bottom of the perforation by weaving over one, under two from the left, inner side.

Weave over one, under two from the right.

FIGURE 44. Hat of open-weave hat braid, trimmed with two-strand trimming band and
fuchia ornament made of shredded palmetto. For detail of braid, see Figure 43, p. 61.

Reach under strands 1, 2, and 3 on the left, grasp strand 4 and weave it under strand 3, over strand 2, under *and back over strand 1*, under strand 2, over strand 3, and under one, over one, under two.

Weave over one, under two from the right. With strand 1 weave over one, under one, over one, under one, over one, and under two from the left.

Weave over one, under two from the right. With strand 2 weave over one, under one, over one, under one,

over one, under two from the left.

Weave over one, under two from the right. With strand 3 weave over one, under one, over one, under one, over one, and under two from the left.* Repeat procedure between stars (*).

Strand 4 is so manipulated that it forms a part of the back edge and the entire front edge of the triangular perforation. It is placed so as to be on the rise of the scallop and is not meant to be on a level with the creases in strands 1, 2, and 3, which make the

58

FIGURE 46. Large garden hat of combination hat braid trimmed with a flower made of palmetto fronds and leaves of palmetto fiber. Easily made braid and makes up attractively.

upper edge of the scallop and form the rest of the lace stripe. These should be sharply creased at the upper edge to make a firm, even-top scallop.

Other points to observe: A firm even base braid; two turns to form the bottom of the perforation; the unusual up-and-down movement of strand 4; a straight-edge scallop; and an even lace stripe.

FISHPOT BRAID
(Fig. 47AB)

This lovely example takes its homely name from the fishtrap made with the same weave by Atlantic islanders. It is really a simple weave, though a bit puzzling until it is mastered, and makes a particularly attractive lightweight, sturdy hat. Any even number of strands from six up may be used, but this braid should never be attempted with strands wider than ⅛ inch. As in all braids, the right routine must be established, and particular attention be given to detail at the right moment.

CAUTION: Do not make the mistake of tightening the button too much, as this is essentially an open weave and overtightness hinders manipulation of strands. Points, however, should be

59

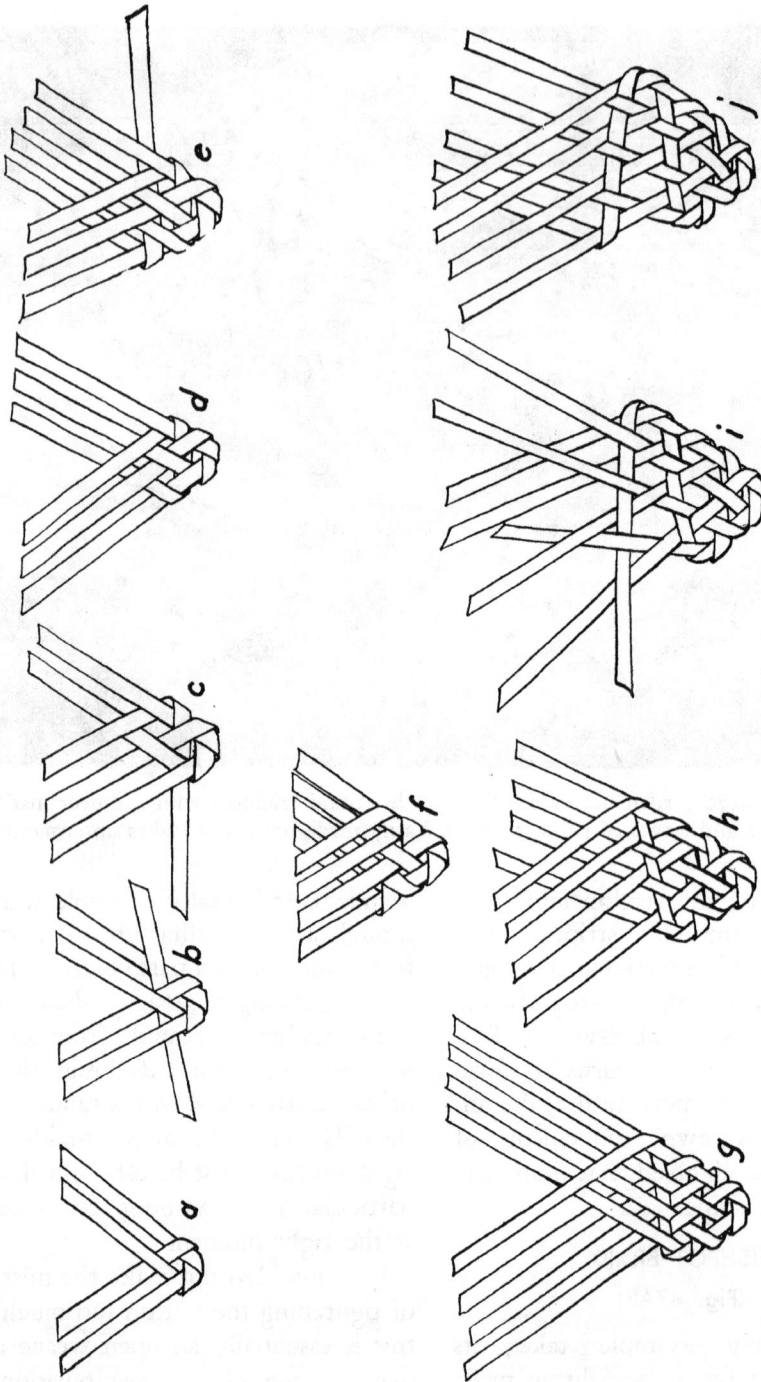

FIGURE 47A. Detail of fishpot braid; *a* through *j* show step-by-step procedure. Figure 48 shows a hat constructed of this braid—a light, lovely, lacy, garden hat.

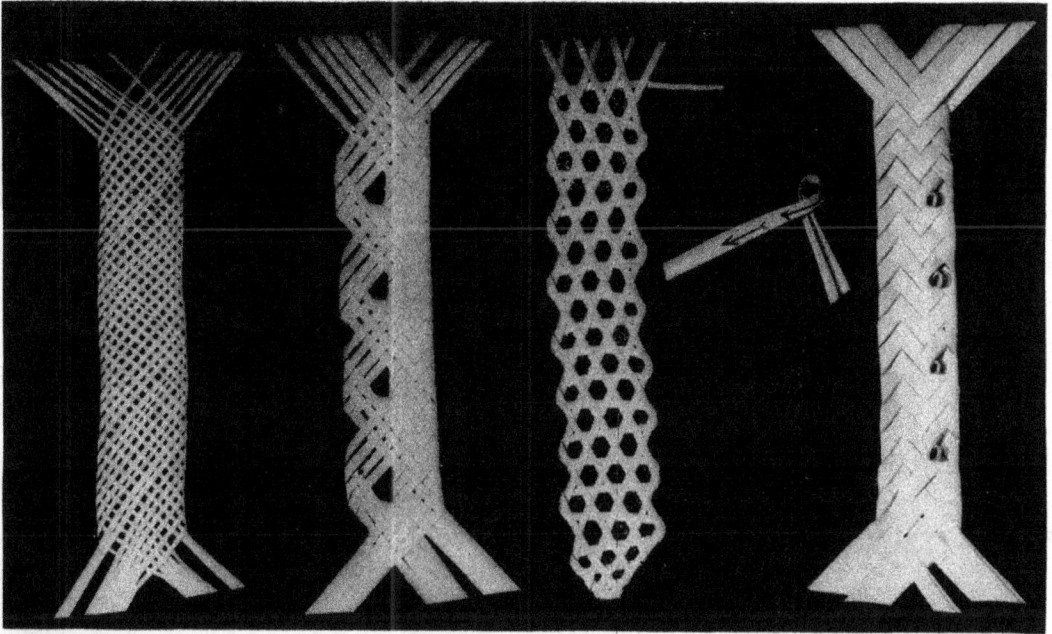

Fig. 43   Fig. 45   Fig. 47B Fig. 49B-*a* Fig. 49B-*b*

FIGURE 43. Open-weave hat braid constructed of fifteen strands woven in check weave. See Figure 44. FIGURE 45. Combination-weave hat braid. See Figure 46. FIGURE 47B. Sample of the fishpot braid. For hat of this weave, see Figure 48. FIGURE 49B-*a*. Detail of curl in construction of goose-eye braid. *b*. Sample of the goose-eye braid.

tight enough to be sharp and regular.

Make a button as in Chapter III, using two strands a scant ⅛ inch wide. Fig. 47A-*a*.

Lay a third strand across the back of the button, and bring the right end up between strands 1 and 2 on the right. Fig. 47A-*b*. Carry this strand back down over strand 1 and up between strands 1 and 2 again, where it overlays strand 2. Fig. 47A-*c*.

Bring the left end of this third strand up over the left outside strand and weave it under two strands. Fig. 47A-*d*.

Lay another strand across the back of the braid, bring the left end up between strands 1 and 2 on the left, carry it back down over strand 1, and lay parallel the strands pointing right. Fig. 47A-*e*. Bring the right end of this strand up over the outside right strand and lay parallel the strands pointing left. Fig. 47A-*f*. This procedure results in an eight-strand layout.

Weaving is accomplished in this braid by one weaver in horizontal progress across the braid *over* the spokes which slant from right to left and *under* those which slant from left to right. The weaver rests in the

61

FIGURE 48. A large, lacy hat constructed of fishpot braid.

crotches of the spokes where they cross and is used across once only, after which it goes into the weave and its place as weaver is taken by the next outer strand on the same side.

* Turn the outer left strand down neatly under the first left-to-right spoke, up over the adjacent right-to-left spoke, under the second left-to-right spoke, over the second right-to-left spoke, under the third left-to-right spoke, over the outer right-to-left spoke, under and back up over the outside right spoke, where it be-

comes a right-to-left spoke. Fig. 47A-*g*.

The right-to-left spokes all lap over the left-to-right spokes but must be so arranged after each passage of the weaver across the braid. Fig. 47A-*h*. This forms three distinct crosses in an eight-strand braid.

Turn the outer strand on the right directly across the braid, forming a neat point by folding it over the left leg of the outside right cross, and weave under one, over one, under one, over one, under one, over one,

62

which leaves the weaver sticking straight out at the left edge of the braid. Fig. 47A-*i*. Make the lower half of the left point by folding this strand under the left, outside, right-to-left strand closely so that it lies parallel the left-to-right strands. Arrange right-to-left overcrosses.* Fig 47A-*j*. Repeat procedure between stars (*). Splice on the horizontal.

See hat constructed of this braid in Fig. 48.

GOOSE-EYE BRAID, HERRINGBONE BASE
(Fig. 49AB, pp. 61, 63)

This braid is made double—that is, one strand on another—as, so braided, it is particularly good for a sturdy bag or basket, and the pattern is such that no ornamentation is required. Contrast, if desired, may be secured by a plain, herringbone band, of which the bottom and handles should be fashioned. See Figs. 50-*a* and 50-*b*.

Using fourteen strands so placed as to form seven strands, weave them into each other at undivided butt ends, check weave. Divide so as to have four strands pointing right, three pointing left.

Weave over one, under two from both right and left three times to establish the herringbone pattern. It will be noted that the usual one long stitch appears in the change from check to herringbone weave.

* Grasp the second strand from the right, and, with a backward motion, make a complete turn. Set the resulting curl, edge up, on the face of the

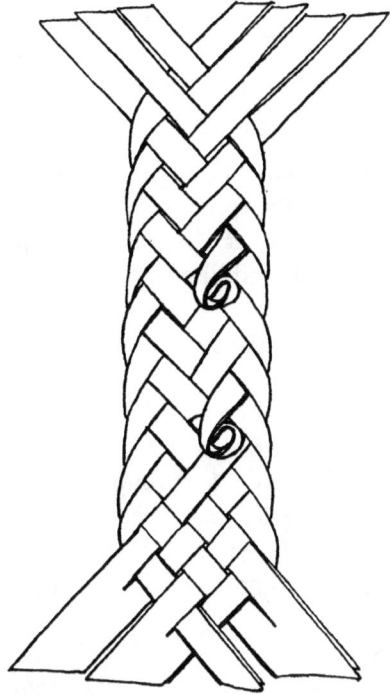

FIGURE 49A. Drawing detail of the attractive goose-eye braid. See bag and basket in Figures 50a and 50b.

braid and hold it in place with the left thumb.

Weave the right outer strand over the curl strand and under two. Weave from the left over one, under two. Hold the curl firmly in place, pull strand to tighten, and weave it over one, under two. Weave from left over one, under two. Weave from both right and left again over one, under two.* Repeat procedure between stars (*).

Note that the curl is a trifle to the right of center and that there are two herringbone stitches between each curl. Keep the braid very firm and the edges true. Splicing should be done singly so as to avoid excess bulk.

FOUR-STRAND FISHTAIL BRAID
(Figs. 51, 52, pp. 66, 67)

This braid, though seemingly intricate, is really quite simple. The best way to master it is by using strips of paper numbered like Fig. 51-a and follow the instructions exactly. It is a braid that lends itself to the construction of a wide variety of articles ranging from belts to rugs.

Make a button as in Chapter III and number strands 1 through 4, beginning at the left and being sure that ends are uneven, in order that splicings will come at inequal intervals. Fig. 51-a.

The strands for this braid are usually ⅜ inch to ½ inch wide, though, for a trimming band, ⅛-inch strands make for daintiness.

* Holding the double V between the thumb and second finger of each hand, flip strands 1 and 3 forward by slipping the index finger of the left hand behind them and stroking them forward over the left thumb.

Fold strand 4 over strand 2 behind strands 1 and 3, which finishes the point on the right side. Fig. 51-b. Draw strand tight, straight across the braid. Allow strands 1 and 3 to fall back to position.

Fold strand 4 over strand 1 and weave, or pass under strand 2, which finishes the movement of strand 4 across the braid, Fig. 51-c, during which process it finished the point on the right, made the lower half of the

point on the left, and restored the double-V figure which is between the completion of every half point.

With the right index finger, flip forward strands 2 and 3 and fold 1 over 4 behind them, Fig. 51-d, making the upper half of the point on the left. Draw the strand tight at this point. No tightening of the upper half of the point is possible later.

Complete the movement by folding 1 over 3 and weave or pass under 4. Fig. 51-e. This makes the upper half of the point on the left and the first half of the point on the right, and restores the double-V figure.* Repeat procedure between stars (*). Proceed, making points on alternate sides in this manner.

This braid cannot be tightened by the method used in check and herringbone weaves. Instead it is made tight by creasing the folds cleanly along the edges of the strands over which they are made, by folding the horizontal strands so that their lower edges form a straight line, and by giving a sharp tug to the upright end of the strand which forms the lower half of a point. Keep points clean cut.

In order to keep the braid an even width, splicing must be done before the strand narrows, and it must be done on the vertical. A horizontal splice will not hold.

To SPLICE: Cut the butt end of the new strand on such an angle that it will fit the edge of a point. Run it down behind the strand to be spliced and into the pocket on the edge of the braid where the last point was made

FIGURE 50-*a*. Bag made of goose-eye braid. Yardage depends upon size of basket or bag desired. This basket has the plain herringbone-braid handles, and the bottom of the bag is made of the plain braid. *b*. Sewing basket constructed of goose-eye braid with the knob on the cover made of push-and-pull braid sewed side up. The bottom of the basket is plain herringbone braid. *c*. Bag constructed of six-strand fishtail braid, underside of the braid to the outside of the bag. A combination of colored and natural strands is used. *d*. Square box with cover, woven over a dummy. Instructions for making are included in Chapter XI.

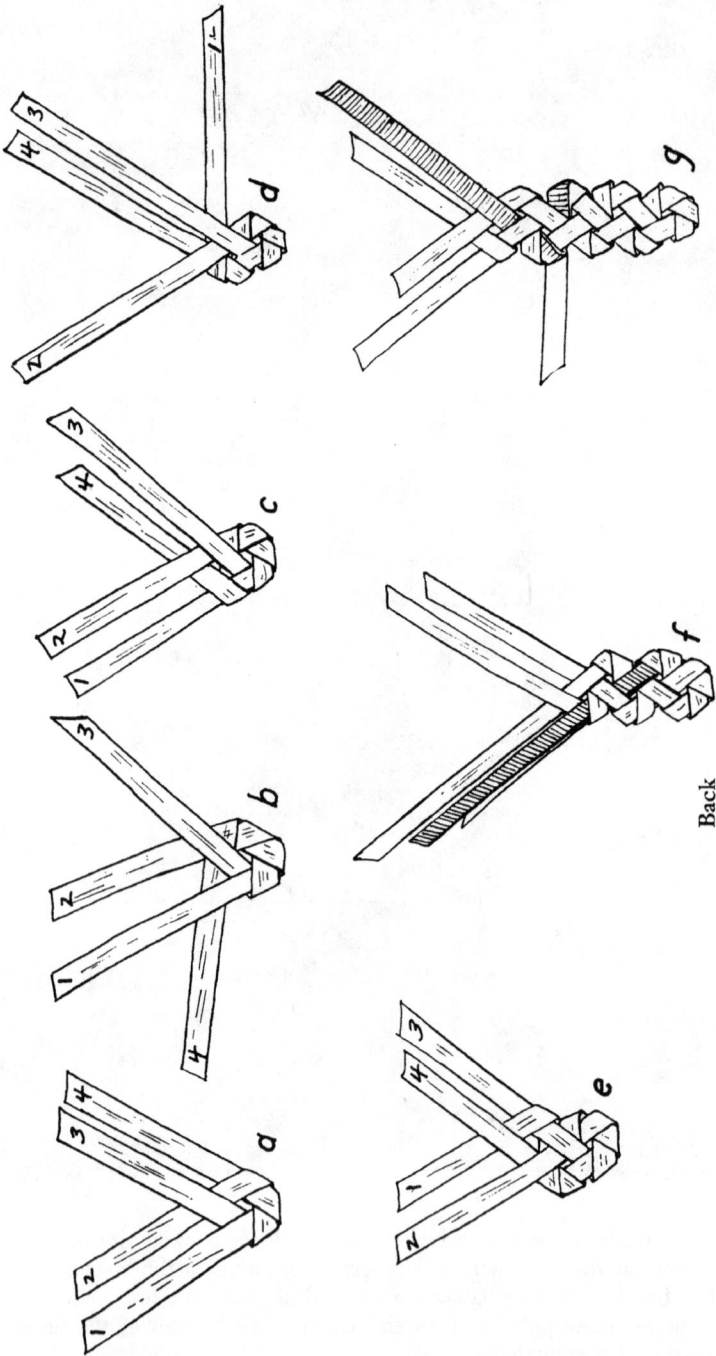

Back

FIGURE 51. Step-by-step procedure in braiding four-strand fishtail braid.

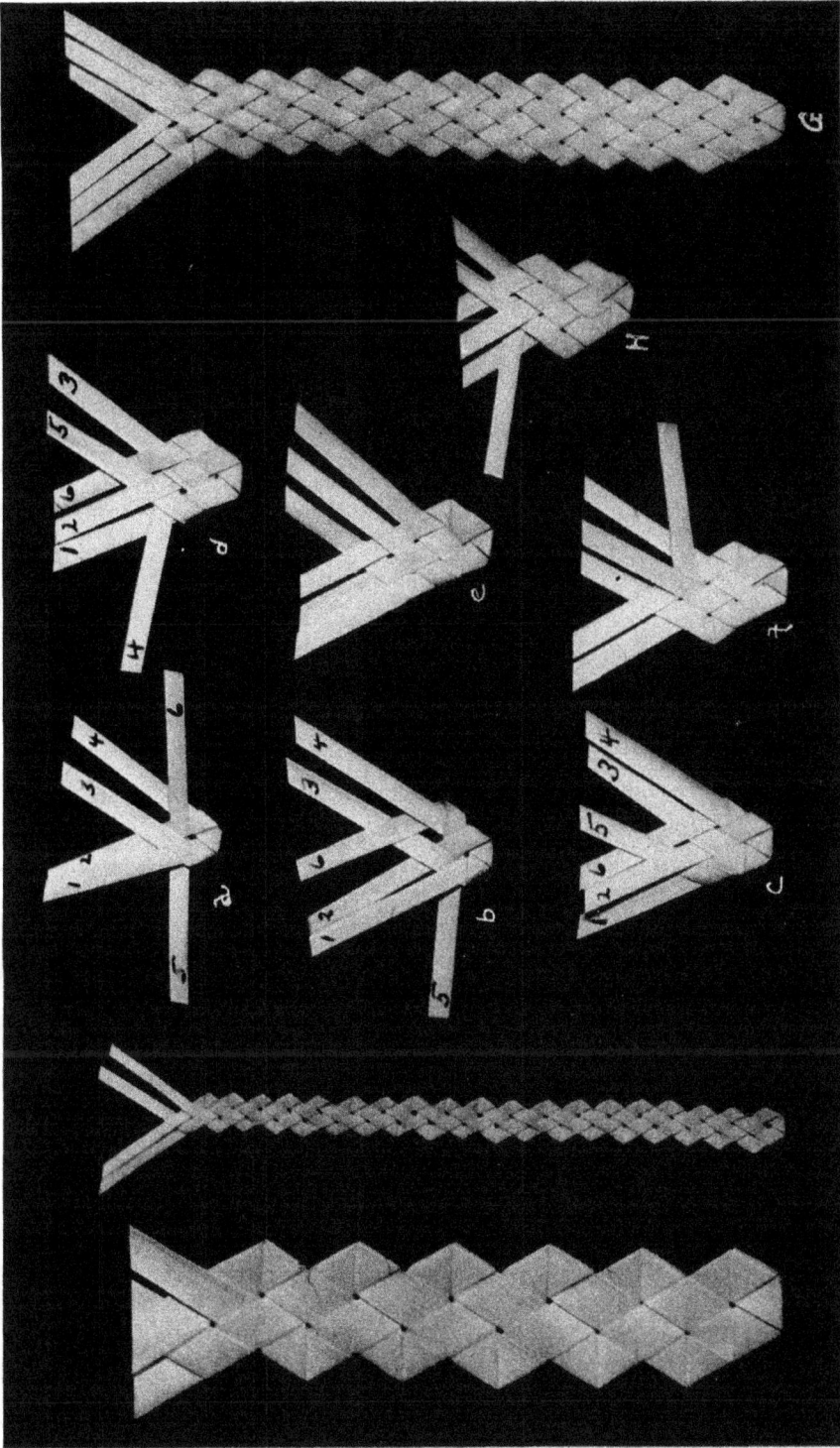

Fig. 52-a

Fig. 52-b

Fig. 53

FIGURE 52-a. Sample of four-strand fishtail braid. This wide width is used in rugs and coarser articles. b. Sample of four-strand fishtail braid using narrow or fine weavers. Suitable for trimming bands. FIGURE 53. Details showing step-by-step procedure in the braiding of the six-strand fishtail braid; G shows how the finished braid looks.

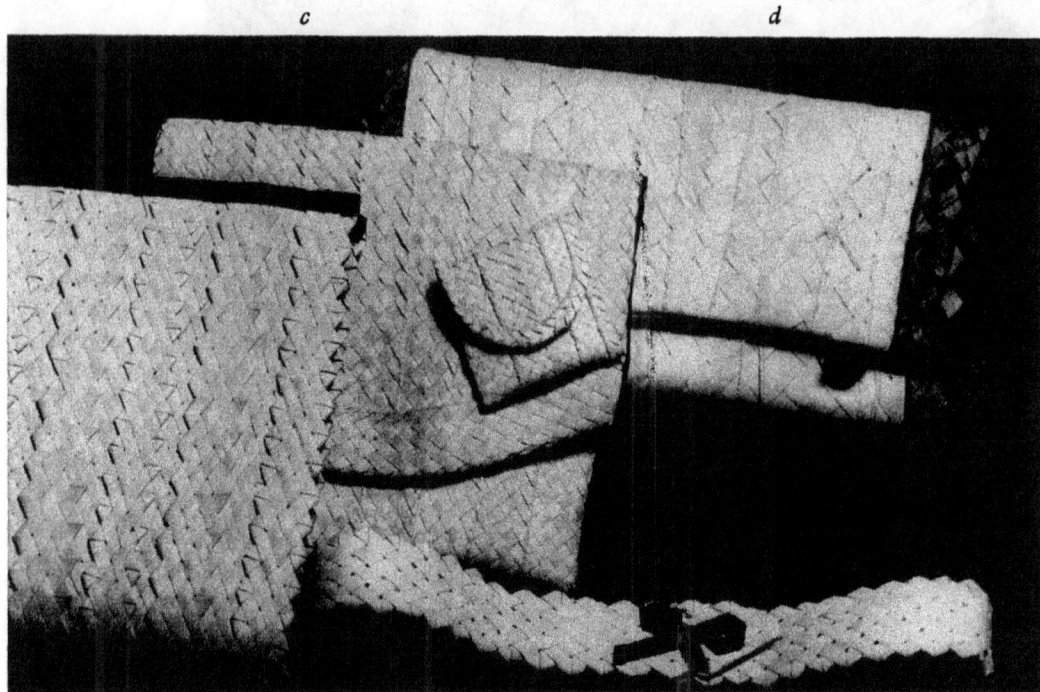

c   *d*

a   *b*

FIGURE 54-*a*. Handbag made of overlapping, six-strand fishtail braid and bound with grosgrain ribbon. *b*. Belt made of six-strand fishtail braid and trimmed with grosgrain ribbon. *c*. Underarm bag and coin purse made of check-weave braid. Large bag has trimming band of curve-edge braid on flat. *d*. Underarm bag in two colors. Made of simple check weave but beginning the braid with the wide end of the strand and braiding through to the tapering end, thus making the braid wider at one end than the other. Overlapping the narrow ends over the wide ends makes a bag that is interesting and sturdy in design. Buttons are dyed *Cocus plumosus* palm seed.

with that strand. Fig. 51-*f*. Work the old and the new strands as one until a half point has been turned. This turn will make the splice secure. Drop the old strand which with the new strand at this point sticks out at right angles from the braid, Fig. 51-*g*, and proceed with the braiding, using the new strand. The old strand should be trimmed off on the back close to the edge of the center check. There will be less waste, and a longer strand may

be secured for a wide braid, if material for this braid is cut by measure. The frond naturally strips by fiber, so that it runs small sooner than would be the case were it cut. This procedure is not advisable with narrow strands but is decidedly the best method with from ⅜-inch to ½-inch strands. Measure from the straight side of the frond.

Fig. 82-*a* shows this braid as a binding for mats.

SIX-STRAND FISHTAIL BRAID
(Fig. 53)

With two strands ¼ inch wide, make a button as described in Chapter III. Number the ends 1 through 4, beginning at the left. Lay another strand (the left end to be numbered 5 and the right end 6) across the back of the button, Fig. 53-*a*, and bring 6 up between 3 and 4, back behind strand 4, up again between strands 3 and 4, and allow to fall over 3. Fig. 53-*b*. Turn end 5 up over strand 1; weave under 2 and over 6. Fig. 53-*c*. This forms a triple V.

* Fold the extreme outside right strand back over strand 6, so forming a point, pass across the back of the braid, up between the first and second outer strands on the left, Fig. 53-*d*, down over the outside strand, back between the first and second outer strands, and up into the weave. Fig. 53-*e*. Fold outside left strand down over the strand just woven, finishing a point on the left. Pass the strand across the back of the braid, up between the first and second outer strands on the right, Fig. 53-*f*, over and down under the outside right strand, and back up and into the weave.* Repeat procedure between stars. Fig. 53-*h* shows the beginning of a new point after the manipulations described in the text between the stars (*) have been completed. Fig. 53-*g* shows a sample of this braid.

The outer strands form points on the sides. The first half of a point is made by folding under and back up, the second half by folding another strand under and across the braid. Tighten by giving a pull on the strand which forms the lower half of the point. Keep points sharply turned. Note that there is no point formed at the left side by end numbered 5. This is omitted to establish the order of a point between the opposite two points. Any even number of strands may be used for this braid.

Splice lengthwise of the braid as in the four-strand fishtail braid, but on the front, as the turn is to the back. This will cover the end of the old strand. Crosswise splicing rarely holds. Trim off the old strand so that it fits neatly in under the strand passing from side to side across the back.

Suitable for belts, bags or decorative bands. Figs. 50-*c* and 54-*a-b*.

Chapter VII

TRIMMING BANDS

THE FOLLOWING braids are not difficult to make and are essential where palmetto products require a natural trimming. Some of the braids can be used for handles, for bracelets, bands, and other things where a single band of braid is desired. See Figs. 55–60.

TWO-STRAND TRIMMING BAND

Reminiscent of kindergarten days is this simplest of all braiding, which is really not braiding but folding. It has, however, a real place as a trimming band and is without a successful rival when made with one strand in order to give a finished end for the center and stem-in-one for tubular palmetto flowers.

With a strand $\frac{3}{16}$ inch wide, form a V with the left leg under. Fold left over right, which makes a sharp point. Proceed, using alternate strands and folding an edge flat over that adjacent to it, creasing sharply and holding the accumulated folds between the thumb and index finger of the left hand until they become bulky. Release some of the braid and repeat the procedure until the desired length is made.

Splice by slipping a new, square-cut, end strand under the old strand, which leave uncut until several folds have made the new strand secure.

THREE-STRAND TRIMMING BAND

A braid adaptable to many uses and dignified by its simplicity.

Prepare three strands $\frac{3}{16}$ inch wide, two of them undivided at the butt end. Lay the butt end of the third strand in this division in the frond, over the left and under the right strand, leaving only enough of the strand protruding on the left side to make the end secure. Fig. 56A-*a*.

Fold the right end of this third strand over both vertical strands so that it points left at a sharp, downward angle. Fig. 56A-*b*. Tension plays a large part in the success of this braid. It is held by the thumb and fingers of the left hand over the left forefinger throughout the braiding, which is done entirely with the right hand.

* Fold the outer left vertical strand to the front down over this strand and pointing right so that the fold follows the upper edge of the angled strand pointing left. Fig. 56A-*c*. Fold the angled strand pointing left up over the angled strand pointing right so that it parallels the right vertical

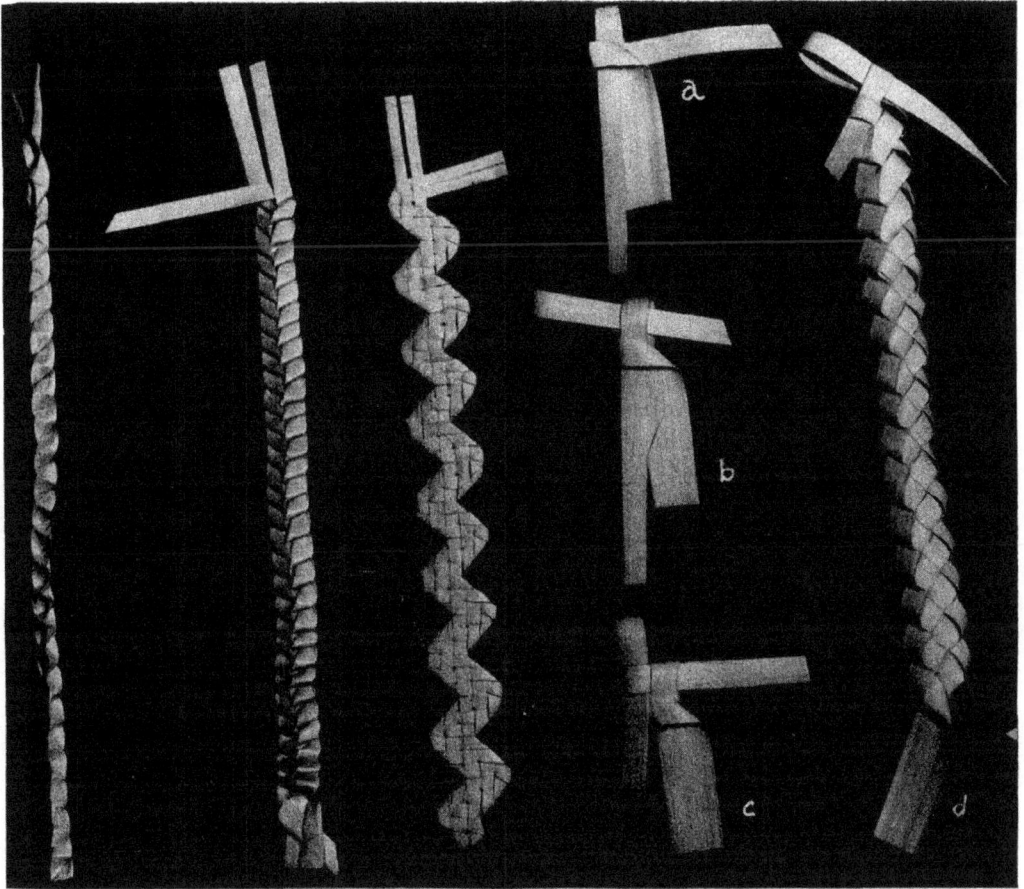

FIGURE 55. Sample of two-strand trimming band. FIGURE 56B. Sample of three-strand trimming band. FIGURE 57. Sample of rickrack braid. FIGURE 58. Detail of push-and-pull braid.

Fig. 55   Fig. 56B   Fig. 57   58

strand. Fig. 56A-d. Fold the right vertical strand to the left so that the fold follows the upper edge of the angled strand. Fig. 56A-e. Fold the angled strand pointing right so as to restore the parallel vertical figure which is between every completed stitch. Repeat procedure between stars (*). Fig. 56A-g. is a length of the braid completed. Fig. 56B is a photographic sample of this braid.

To complete a stitch, there are two movements from the same side, one across the braid, the other in such a manner as to restore the parallel vertical. The angle at which the outer strands are folded controls the symmetry of the braid. Angle strands,

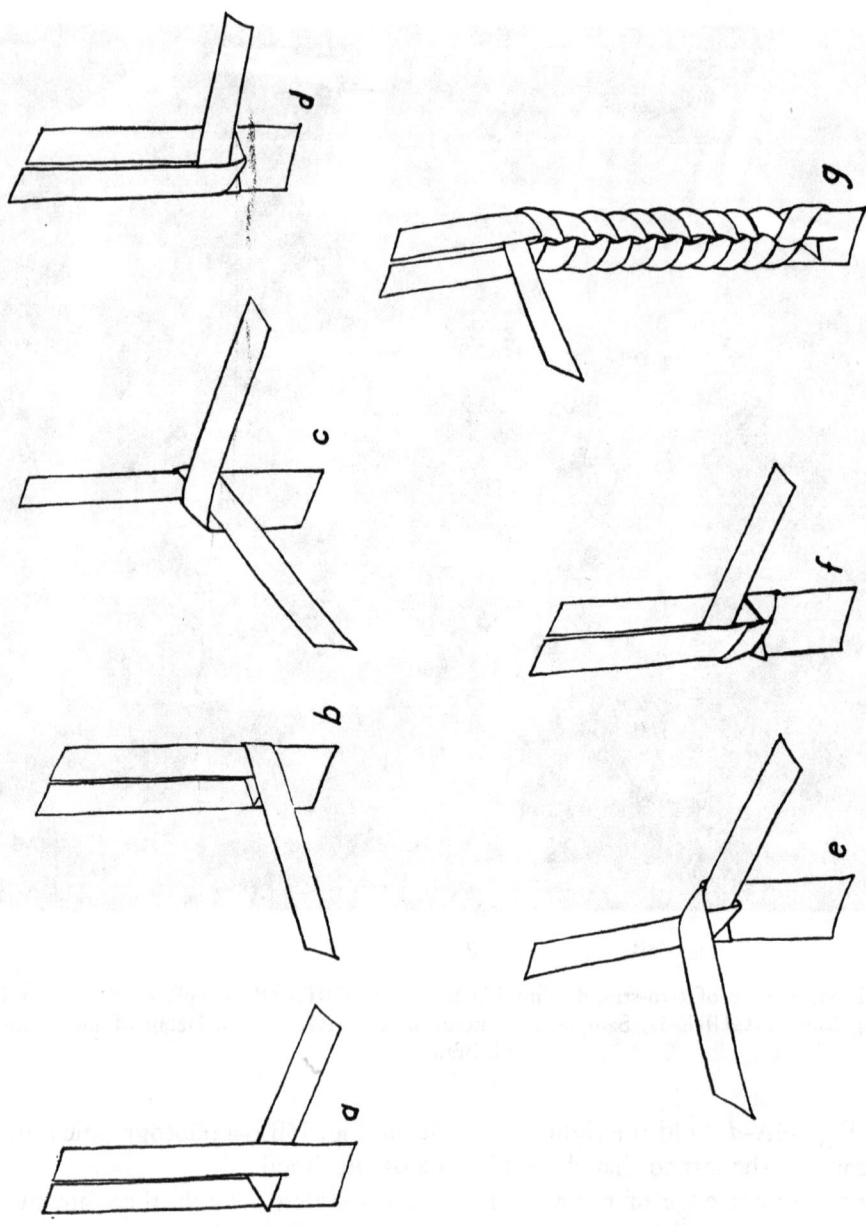

FIGURE 56A. Step-by-step procedure in braiding the three-strand trimming band.

when in position, should be just short of a right angle so that the outer lower edge comes to the upper tip of the last completed stitch on the opposite side. This will leave only a small, unequal-sided triangle showing between the lower edge of the strand in use and the last completed stitch. Fig. 56A-f.

Splicings should be done on the back by slipping a new strand, the end cut on an angle into a finished stitch just below the strand to be spliced. For security, give the old strand two folds in the braiding before cutting it off.

RICKRACK TRIMMING BAND, CHECK WEAVE

Using two strands ⅛ inch wide, make a button as in Chapter III. Weave over one from the right.

* With the remaining strand pointing right, weave over one, under one, over one, which places this strand directly across the other strands and pointing left.

Weave outer right strand over one, under one. Weave the next outer strand on the right over one. This places three strands pointing left across strand 1, which is the outer left strand of the button, the stay strand. Weave the lower left strand under one, over one. Weave the next left strand under one. This places these strands parallel with strand 1. Note that all strands lie alternately across then parallel strand 1. Fig. 57, p. 71.

With the remaining strand pointing left, weave under one, over one, under one straight across all strands so that it points right. Follow with the left outer strand, weaving under one, over one. Weave the next outer strand on the left under one so that all three strands are at right angles to strand 1.

Weave over one, under one with the lowest right strand. Weave over one with next higher right strand so that both are parallel with strand 1.* Repeat procedure between stars (*).

Strand 1 does not change position. It is the backbone of the braid and is used to get symmetry. A slight pull on the end of it will prove its effectiveness in this respect.

PUSH-AND-PULL BRAID
(Fig. 58, p. 71)

Prepare two strands ¼ inch wide, undivided at the butt end. Make a short loop on the left by turning the strand back on itself, tip over butt to the front. Wrap the right strand over this loop and bring it around to the right side. Fig. 58-a.

* Make a loop with the right strand by folding it back over itself to the front, insert the right loop through the left loop snugly, and pull the left loop down tight. Fig. 58-b.

Make a loop with the left strand by folding it back on itself to the front, insert it through the right loop snugly, and pull the right strand tight.* Fig. 58-c. Repeat procedure between stars (*). Fig. 58-d shows a finished sample of this braid. Do not crease. All turns should be curved and of equal tightness.

Splicing is accomplished by inserting a new strand into the last loop

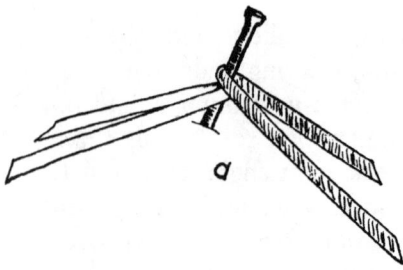

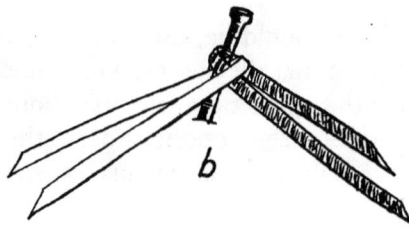

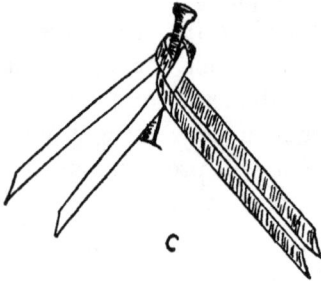

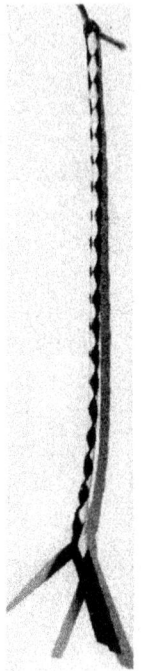

Fig. 59A

Fig. 59B

FIGURE 59. Details *a* through *d* show procedure in braiding four-strand round braid, useful in making handles and trimmings.

made by the strand to be spliced, then inserting both strands through the opposite loop. The old strand is then cut off on the under side.

This is one of the old trimming bands. Easy to make and quite decorative.

FOUR-STRAND ROUND BRAID
(Fig. 59AB)

This braid is indispensable to the palmetto worker, as it is unexcelled for fastenings and handles. It may be small enough for a belt loop, about ⅛ inch in diameter, or large enough to handle a heavy basket, usually about an inch in diameter. Any round braid larger than ⅛ inch in diameter should

be reinforced—that is, made around a core. The lack of this detail, even in a handle of ¼ inch diameter, results in a creased or broken cord.

Select two long strands of palmetto of the same size but of different colors. The development of four sets of diamonds enables the beginner to hold the braiding pattern more easily. Choose a color for each hand and keep that color in the same hand throughout. A change results in a lost pattern.

For clarity, these directions are given by crosshatched or colored strands. After the routine is mastered, the braider will have no difficulty with a one-color braid.

Drive a nail straight up into a flat

74

surface, such as a shelf, of any convenient height. The nail should be placed near the edge to avoid interference in grasping the material to be braided closely. Loop around it, unevenly, for the sake of splicings, a strand of blue palmetto for the right hand and a strand of natural palmetto for the left. Figure 59-*a*. Slip the inside natural strand under and fold it up over the inside blue strand. Figure 59-*b*.

* Slip the outside blue strand under the inside blue and inside natural strands and fold it up over the inside natural strand. Figure 59-*c*. Slip the outside natural strand under the inside natural and inside blue strands and fold it up over the inside blue strand.* Figure 59-*d*. Repeat procedure between stars (*).

All weaving is done with the outside strands.

It will be noticed that there is always an outside strand slightly high up on the braid. This is the next weaver and is important in a one-tone braid where there are no colors to act as guide. The routine is under two and back over one, working on alternate sides.

The braid should be perfectly round and very firm. The best way to secure this result is to hold the braid closely. If, however, tightening must be done, hold the end of the braid with the thumb and first finger of the left hand and, with the right hand, pull directly down on each strand in succession. If carefully done, this meas-ure will not injure the strands and will take out any looseness.

Splice a weaver where it comes "over one" in the routine. By splicing at this point, the next weaver fastens it twice as it comes "under two" as well as where it folds "over one." The top of the new strand should be trimmed off closely after the braid is finished, but the old strand must be woven with the new one for at least an inch or more (depending on the size of the braid) in order to make it secure.

For a core, secure a soft cord of the desired handle size and, for convenience, fasten the end beyond the nail around which the strands are looped. Allow it to hang down out of the way, but be sure that each strand passes around it snugly at the "under two" step of the braid.

The width of the strand regulates the size of the braid. Strands ¼ inch wide will make a braid of ¼ inch diameter.

See Fig. 66B, basket, and Fig. 78, bottle handles, made of this braid.

FIGURE-EIGHT BRAID
(Fig. 60)

The name of this procedure describes it accurately, as it is achieved by the manipulation of a strand of material as one would make an eight longitudinally over a base, which may be of tough, pliable withes or midrib strippings from palmetto fronds, preferably the latter.

The size of both the base and the width of the weave to be chosen will

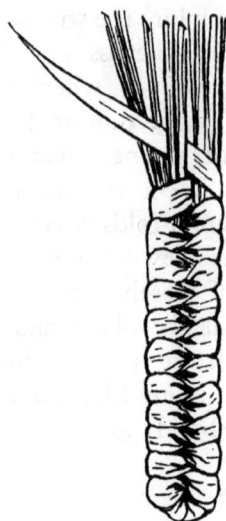

FIGURE 60. Figure-8 braid, useful for handles for baskets.

depend on the weight of the basket to be handled, for this is primarily a handle procedure, though it also is useful as a trimming band for baskets. Six midribs will make a handle of about 3/16 inch thickness and slightly more than ½ inch width. For this size a good ¼ inch weaver is recommended. For a trimming band, a narrower weaver and fewer midribs are advisable.

Arrange six midribs so that the ends are unequal for the sake of necessary splicing, and make an inverted-U

bend in the bundle to one side of the middle for the same reason. Hold the tip end of the weaver in the left hand over the left leg of the ∩ and wrap the bundle tightly for about an inch, up to and just beyond the curve.

* As the weaver comes to the front between the legs of the ∩ from the right, carry it over the left leg and bring it up between the legs to the front, over the right leg, and to the front between the legs.* Repeat procedure between stars (*).

For symmetry, width of the base must be kept constant, and, if made of strippings, splicing must be done at necessary intervals to maintain the thickness.

About every two inches, hold the ends of the base in the right hand and, with the left, pull against the part woven so as to have the edges of the weaver lie tightly against each other and crinkle at the center where it crosses.

Splicing is accomplished by laying the tip end of a new strand under the old weaver an inch or more from the end of the old one and weaving both as one until the old weaver is used up. Trim off ends only after crinkling.

Chapter VIII

BUTTONS

FREQUENTLY buttons or fastenings are needed, particularly in finishing belts, and the following directions may be used to fill this need.

PIGEON-BOX BUTTONS
(Fig. 61)

The ancient procedure known as the "pigeon box" furnishes an excellent button. Two pigeon boxes the same size and a two-inch loop of scant ⅛-inch-diameter, round braid form a practical and appropriate belt fastening.

Five buttons, one large, two medium, and two small, sewed with a short loop of thread on a crocheted cord, make an attractive necklace. They may be used too for dress buttons, though their bulk would render them unsuitable for any but decorative purposes.

For a belt fastening, prepare four strands a good ¼ inch wide or roughly half the width of the button desired and 12 inches to 14 inches long. Though a single button requires only two strands, material for both buttons should be stripped at the same time in order to have the strands of the same width. Fold the strands so as to take advantage of the best width.

Make a V with the left leg under, and lay another strand in the crotch. Number the ends 1 to 4, beginning at the left. Figure 61-*a*.

Fold 4 over 3 and 2 loosely. Fold 2 over 4 and 1 loosely. Fold 1 over 2 and through the crotch of 2 and 3 or the point of the V.

Pull all ends to tighten. This makes a neat little four-patch on the front and a cross on the underside. Fig. 61-*b*. Turn over to put the cross on the top, where it may be woven into the inner part of the button.

Begin at any corner and fold a strand so that it points in the exactly opposite direction. Fasten it down by folding over it the closest strand at a right angle to it. Continue around the button in the same manner and slip the end of the last strand under the first fold made. Weaving is clockwise on the uneven-number layers—that is, on 3 and 5—and counter-clockwise on the even-number layers.

Build up until the button is square —usually about four layers. Trim all ends sharply from left to right, cutting from the ends of the strands. Slip the point into the pigeon box so that

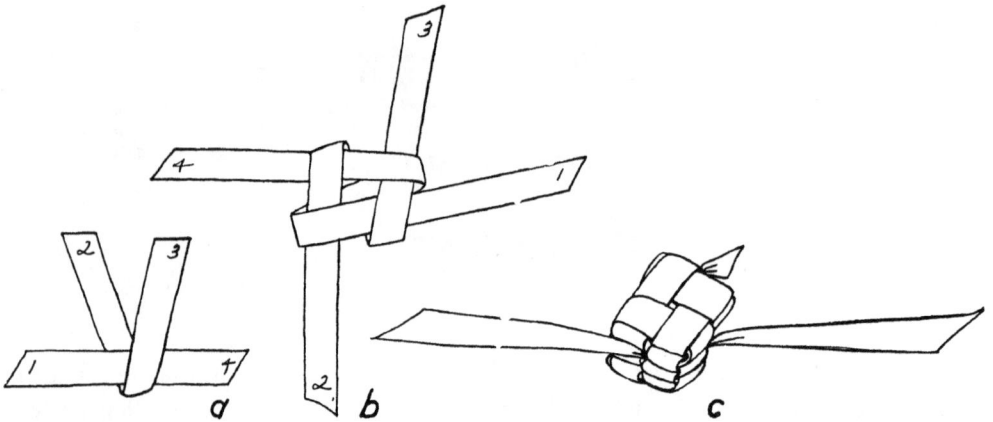

FIGURE 61. Step-by-step procedure in the construction of pigeon-box buttons.

it over weaves the *next-to-the-last* layer, in which position it is almost invisible, and bring it out at the middle of the side. Pull the strand tight and wrench sharply back in order to tighten it in place. Hold it in this position while the next strand is woven back in. Wrench it back also, and hold the ends while the remaining strands are woven in. Fig. 61-c.

Trim the ends square, barely long enough to reach the corner toward which they point. In a half-inch-width button, this will mean an end a scant ¼ inch long. With the point of the scissors, grasp the side of the end and push it into the pigeon box, one on each of the four sides.

Sew both ends of the round braid loop about an inch and a half from the point of the belt, and cover by sewing a button over them. Sewing may be done invisibly by bringing the point of the needle up through the exact center of the button and carrying it back through the center so that the thread does not remain on the outside layer. Sew the second button back from the left end so that the right end laps over the left when the loop is in place around the button.

OTHER BUTTON OR TRIMMING SUGGESTIONS

Another button, knob, or rosette may be formed of push-and-pull braid tightly rolled and sewed, side up. The rosette appears on the purse in Fig. 1 showing "styles of the seventies." The knob is very effective on the round, covered goose-eye basket. See Fig. 50-b.

Chapter IX

PATTERN POSSIBILITIES BY COLOR COMBINATIONS

THE fact that palmetto frond is highly repellent to ordinary dyes has, until fairly recently, restricted its use by braiders to the natural-color product. As a consequence, they had to depend on achieving patterns through variations in weaves, and it is likely that this handicap was largely responsible for stimulating originality and resulted in many more patterns being created than otherwise would have been. See Fig. 62.

There are now on the market penetrative dyes in a range of lovely colors which the palmetto frond (and probably other materials discussed) will take, but most of these dyes are, as yet, quite expensive and the dying process is somewhat tedious even with the proper equipment, as the frond must be held in a vat of dye solution until thoroughly impregnated with color so that there are no white edges to show when it is stripped. The necessary drying then takes about as long as the original curing.

Fortunately, it is possible to buy the palmetto frond dyed, and a few strands of color add variety and piquancy even to the simplest weaves. In fact, the plain, contrasting braids display the color to the greatest advantage.

If a central motif is desired, the weave must be of an even-strand check. An eight-strand weave of the four center strands in color, two each pointing right and left, with two natural or contrasting strands on each side, will result in a pattern of colored diamonds outlined by triangles of contrast. Fewer strands result in a smaller diamond or a smaller triangle, as one wills. Fig. 62-*a*.

Spectacular plaids are possible in wide braids, but, for best results, a strong color accent must be included in the weave. Experimentation will prove that the possibilities are limitless. Fig. 62-*b*. Even the plainest five-strand, check-weave braid can make an unusual belt with bias color pattern if strands of light color, a very strong-colored one, and a slightly less strong-colored contrasting one are arranged pointing right, with another strand of the strong color and another one of the light color woven in pointing left. This arrangement puts the light-color strands on the outer edges. Fig. 62-*c*. For such patterns, best results are obtained with check weaves, as the her-

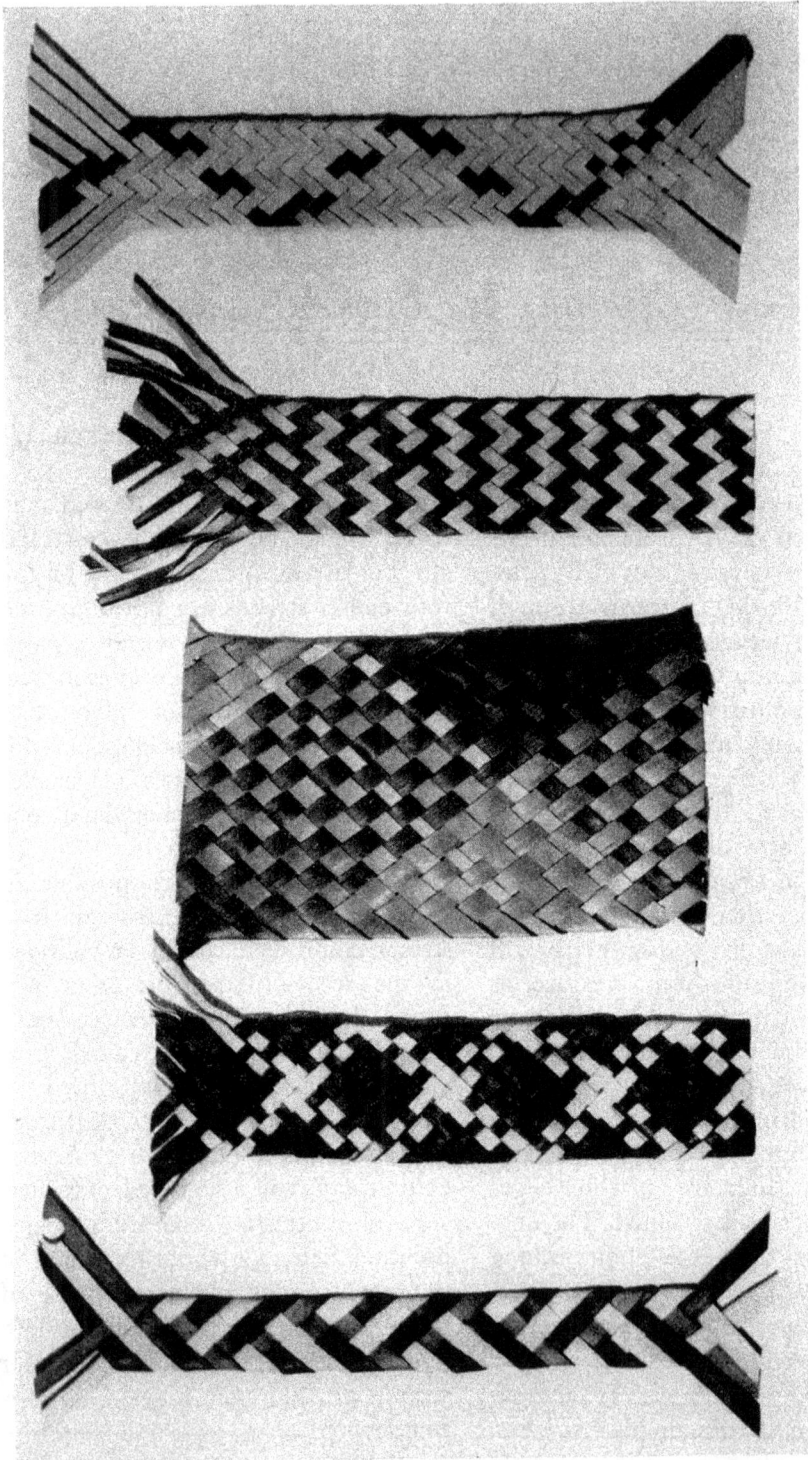

FIGURE 62. *See special note, p. 81*

a   b   c   d   e

ringbone weave has the limitation of long stitches. The classic use of color in herringbone weave is nine strands of natural frond with two strands of color laid in parallel. This results in a zigzag pattern up the braid which has an air of restrained dignity. Fig. 62-*d*. Also see Fig. 63, handbag, and Fig. 65-*a*, a book cover.

One will frequently see in the imported handbags a trimming band which looks as if it were made up of crosswise strips of rickrack braid. This is simply a herringbone, usually of fifteen strands, made of alternate natural and colored strands. There is an unavoidable flaw at certain intervals near the edges which is less noticeable if the two outer strands are of the natural color, that is, eight strands of natural and seven strands of color. Fig. 62-*e*.

Handbags of distinction may be made by use of discriminating combinations of contrasting color braids sewed together. These, of course, should be plain, flat braids in either check or herringbone pattern. Fig. 64.

Fancy-edge hat braids in color are charming if confined to a single tone. Varicolored strands are likely to give a Joseph's-coat effect.

Fishtail braids are especially fine for belts but they do not lend themselves well to color combinations in the weave owing to their manner of construction. They are lovely if made in one tone.

The round braid of "trimming bands," Chapter VII, is not only more decorative when made of two colors, which, in the weave, show up as four rows of diamonds, but they also serve as guide for the beginner and make the learning of this pattern much easier.

FIGURE 62. Pattern possibilities by color combinations. *a*. Even-strand check weave of diamond and triangle pattern. Twelve strands were used in this sample instead of the eight strands mentioned in the text. The eight-strand braid would be of smaller diamonds and triangles. *b*. Check weave of nineteen strands arranged with one yellow, eight blue strands pointing right; one blue, four red, two green, one yellow, and two green strands pointing left. This combination makes a striking plaid. *c*. Five-strand check weave, using dark brown, light brown, and a natural strand pointing right, a natural and dark brown strand pointing left. An interesting pattern. *d*. Herringbone weave using nine strands of natural and two of colored material. Figure 63 shows this pattern of braid sewed together to form a striking pattern in a round handbag. Figure 65-*a* shows a book cover in a like pattern. *e*. A fifteen-strand herringbone braid using alternate and colored strands. This gives the appearance of rickrack.

FIGURE 63. Fifteen-strand herringbone braid constructed of three strands of brown and twelve strands of natural palmetto. A commercial pattern was used both for proportions and construction. The braid is put together so that the diamond pattern is produced by joining the brown at the edges. Inset shows enlarged design.

Chapter X

THE SEWING OF BRAIDS

NOTE: *Always moisten braid. Never try to work dry braid. Take care not to have too wet. Best plan: wet it lightly, then wrap in a heavy towel or cloth for several hours before working.*

Proficiency in the sewing together of braids is acquired by practice, so it is recommended that sufficient yardage of the basic braids be made to provide practice both for braiding and for sewing.

Stitching may be done by machine, lapping the edges of the braid and using a long stitch, or by hand, using invisible stitching at least on the right side through lapped edges of slightly moistened braid.

Braids may also be fastened together securely by lacing or running a soft, strong twine, tape, or other lacer through every other check in alternate edges of the braids to be fastened together. Pulled taut, the lacer does not show.

Variation with plain-edge braids is secured by the method of lapping, which may be one edge over the other either from the right or left. A band may be placed in the middle of the pattern and the lapping made to follow its edge, to the right on one side and to the left on the other. Alternate bands may be lapped over alternate underbands. This is a particularly good method for fishtail braids, for braids with fancy edges, and for narrow underbands which may join together bands of another size either of braid width or strand width. See book covers, Fig. 65-a-b; six-strand fishtail workbag, Fig. 50-c; and underarm purse, Fig. 54-a. Also large shopping bag, herringbone weave, Fig. 16.

It is well to remember that anything is permissible which looks as if one intended it to be that way.

For beginners a flat project such as an envelope purse or a book cover is preferable, as such articles present the minimum difficulty.

A PURSE OR UNDERARM BAG

Determine the size desired by experimenting with a folded paper to get width and length of the purse and shape and width of the lap. Cut and open out the pattern flat. Commercial patterns are available in every pattern department and perhaps are better for the amateur because of the experience the patternmaker has had with pro-

FIGURE 64. Shopping bag of seven-strand and underarm bag of eleven-strand herringbone braid, using a combination of dyed and natural palmetto in a set rotation. Braid is started in one color and eight to twelve inches woven; then another color is braided onto that for the same length, and so on, until braid of sufficient length is made. Bags are sewed together, following directions in sewing instructions. Yardage depends on width of strand and number of strands in braid.

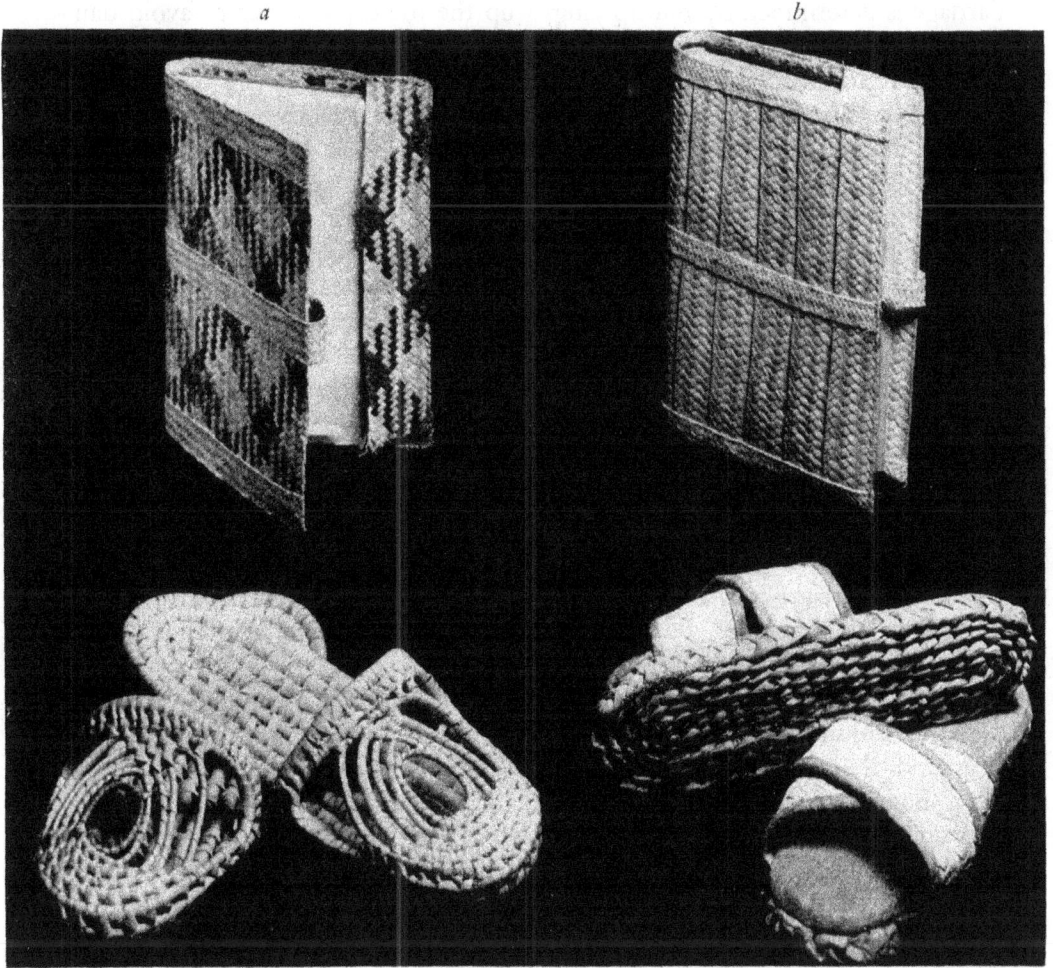

FIGURE 65-*a*. A book cover in two colors in herringbone weave. *b*. A book cover in this weave using a coarse and fine braid. Both of these were stitched on the sewing machine. *c*. Slides of coiled palmetto. These would be just as effective if made of bear grass, yucca, mulberry root, cattail rush, corn shucks, or any other strong, pliable fiber. *d*. The soles of this pair of slides are made of braided cattail rush, using a three-strand plait and sewed by coiling with the edges up. The straps across the top are also made of herringbone braid and may be of cattail. The tops of the soles are padded, as are the undersides of the straps, to insure comfort. The sewing of these slides is done by hand. Corn shucks would be excellent for these slides.

portions and the suggestions for style. Yardage is determined by multiplying the length of the open pattern by the number of lengths of braid required to cover the surface of the pattern, allowing, of course, for the minimum lap of edges.

FASTENING ENDS AND CUTTING LENGTHS OF BRAID: Measure off a length of braid, allowing a half inch at each end for seaming. Stitch across the braid and back or sew across the braid with short back stitches to fasten the ends securely. Repeat stitching or sewing about one half inch beyond the first stitching. Cut midway between the stitching. This fastens the ends securely and prevents raveling. The entire yardage may be sewed for cutting in this manner, but cutting should be done only as the progress of the work requires, since lengths put together without regard to the beginning and the ending will present a very hodgepodge appearance. The end which is cut off should be brought back to the beginning of the preceding length so that all folds in braid edges turn the same way. This also makes easier the determining of right and wrong sides.

SEWING: For natural-color palmetto, heavy-duty cotton, color #16 or #18, should be used. If the sewing is done by hand, the thread should be doubled and waxed. Pin two lengths of braid together, lapping the edges ¼ inch or less, placing pins at intervals of two inches or less and at a right angle to the edges of braid. Make an effort to insert the pins between the strands of palmetto which make up the braids, in order to avoid damage. Fasten the end of the thread securely and slip the point of the needle between the strands on the edge of the upper length of braid, down into and through the edge of the lower length of braid; take a stitch and come back to the top, through both braids, bringing the point of the needle through between strands. Insert the needle back between the same strands and slip it along in the folded edge of the upper braid for a stitch and back through both edges to the underside. This method gives a firmly stitched seam with invisible outer stitches and a long, firm understitch. As most of the products fashioned of braids are lined, the long understitches do not show.

Get the habit of pulling the thread tight. This gives a firm fabric and greatly improves the appearance of the finished product.

MACHINE STITCHING: Lap and pin lengths of braid together as for hand sewing. Adjust the stitch to about ⅛ inch and loosen tension slightly. Stitch close to top edge. Should pinning not hold edges true, baste before stitching.

In both hand sewing and machine stitching, measure frequently by the pattern to hold a true straight edge and full size. When the braid covers the pattern, press it under a slightly damp cloth with a mild iron. Trim to square up ends if necessary.

LINING: Cut the lining, which should be of a closely woven, fairly heavy, cotton material (interlining improves the appearance but is optional), with seams on all edges. Fold in the side edges to fit the purse, and baste. Sew the right sides of purse and lining together at the inner top edge of the purse, fastening ends securely. Turn lining and purse-end seam inside. Baste and press with a mild iron. Pull the end of the lining, and baste it to the edge of the flat, making it a scant ⅜ inch shorter than the braid fabric. This will give a snug-fitting lining. Blind-stitch the side edges of the lining to the sides of the purse.

TURNED SEAMS: If turned seams are used, it is always wise to lay the braid between the folds of a damp towel for an hour or so to give the necessary pliability to the palmetto. Do not soak. Excess moisture is undesirable, as it is likely to spot the lining.

SEWING UP: Fold to shape, pin, and blind-stitch the ends of the purse together, fastening the corners securely.

FINISHING FLAP: Bind the end of the flap with an upper and a lower row of braid which should be a single length with the ends brought together on the underside. Sew front edges together after inserting a loop for a fastening, and sew back edges to the purse and the lining.

Another method of binding is the use of a narrower length of braid folded in the middle and stitched in the manner of bias binding. Grosgrain ribbon or a neat cloth binding may be used as a finish around the sides as well as the flap.

For a fastening, use a pierced and polished palm or other seed or a pigeon-box button with the round braid loop of palmetto.

Fill bag neatly with folded newspapers and put under press overnight.

GUSSETS: If gussets are desired, these may be made of a length of braid sewed together with a deep V dart at the inner bottom end to make it hold its fold. Line as described for the inner front edge of the purse, using an inside seam for braid and lining. Sew outer edges to the outer edges of the body of the purse. For a braid binding, fold a narrow braid in the center and bind tops of gussets and inner top edge of purse with a single length of braid.

The method of stitching, as given, places the finished edges of braid on the long edges or sides, leaving the raw edges on the flap and inner front. This is the method most generally used in the construction of purses or underarm bags and has the advantage of holding the length of raw edge to a minimum.

Construction by stitching the braid together from side to side is perfectly legitimate and may be successfully accomplished by stitching a row of narrower braid flat over the raw edges to conceal them or by binding them with a folded narrower braid. The first is a particularly good procedure for a book cover, which needs to lie flat. Pockets for the backs of the book may be fashioned of two rows of braid stitched together and stitched to the cover proper, or a length of braid may be stitched about midway each half of the cover across the inside, through which the book backs may be slipped to hold the book firmly in place.

NOTE: Commercial patterns may be followed throughout without fear.

SHOPPING BAGS: Bags with rounded bottoms are usually made of a continuous length of braid. Calculation of shape and size desired must take into consideration the shape of the bottom and the width of the braid to be used. If the braid is the usual eleven-strand herringbone of about 1¾ inches, three widths of braid will make the oval bottom. A good-sized shopping bag will have about a ten-inch length of braid for a center, and, as in rag rugs, the center does much to control the size and shape of the bag. (See shopping bags of herringbone weave and fishtail braids.)

The braid at the end of this center strip should be eased or pleated in without being cut, so that it may be turned back on itself, pinned, and sewed firmly, the edges pinned under the edge of the center strip and sewed without fullness—using a narrow, lapped seam—to the opposite end of the center length. Fit the braid around this end, easing or pleating it in to make a symmetrical oval. Pin and sew. Continue sewing without fullness except as necessary at the ends of the oval, and begin turning the braid up to form the bag, pinning a few inches and sewing. The shape and size of the bag now being fixed, a pattern should be made of the width and depth from a rectangular piece of heavy cardboard. Round the lower corners

slightly so that the pattern will fit into the oval bottom. Slip this pattern into the work frequently to keep the size and shape of the bag true. Continue pinning and sewing the braid together until the necessary depth has been built up. Taper off the top edge by gradually slipping the inside edge of the braid down in the bag until the top is even. It is well to finish this at a place about two thirds the length of a side so that the end will fall under the band of braid which forms the handle on one side. This band begins at the bottom about one third the length of the oval and is pinned and sewed straight up the side of the bag to the top edge. About eleven inches is allowed for a handle. The braid is then pinned and sewed down the same side at about a third of the width of the bag from the side edge, across the bottom, up the other side, allowance made for a handle, and down the side to the point of beginning.

Fold the lengths left for handles in the center so that the edges meet and blind-stitch them together for six or eight inches.

HATS

The making of hats is possible even for the amateur, but requires considerable patient practice.

It is astonishing, however, what improvement even home blocking can effect, and the results which can be achieved by a professional blocking are truly amazing.

HALO HATS: See Fig. 27-b; also child's hat, Fig. 27-a. These are not at all difficult. If a hat is to be shorter in the back than in front or has any other marked difference in the brim, a commercial hat pattern as nearly as possible a duplicate of the shape desired should be secured. Trace the pattern on heavy paper, but do not cut out.

Pin the braid, which has been slightly moistened, to the heavy paper pattern, outer edge even with the traced outer edge, easing in the fullness of the inner edge and flattening the outer edge. Pin another row of braid over the inner edge of the first row but not through the paper pattern. Remove from pattern and sew the edges together firmly, with as little stitching showing as possible. Continue building the hat in this manner, comparing the work frequently with the paper pattern and smoothing it out well so that it lies flat. In a halo hat with a short back, every row of braid must be cut. Stitch across the braids in two places a half inch apart before cutting between stitching. This will prevent raveling.

When the traced pattern is completely covered, mark the head size with dots through the perforations of the pattern and finish with a length of braid stitched as a finishing band on top of the raw edges along this line of dots. Stitch a head band of ribbon inside, after tacking the finishing band together. Trim with bow and band.

CROWN AND BRIM IN ONE: See Figs. 44, 46, 48. The usual palmetto hat is wide of brim, shallow crowned, and of a lacy weave. Such hats are begun at the center of the crown by folding and pinning an end of braid about an inch long back on itself. The turn is eased and pleated in to form a light oval. Continue easing in and pinning the braid together a few inches in front of the progress of the sewing to form the inverted, saucer-shaped top of the crown. Turn the braid down gradually and build the straight sides of the crown, sewing edge over edge without fulling.

When the desired depth is reached, after being sure that the head size is correct, begin easing in the inner edge to allow for the spread of the brim. Lay on the work table frequently and be sure that sufficient ease has been worked in and pinned before stitching. When the brim reaches the required size, make a symmetrical finish to the edge by slipping the braid back under gradually so that edge meets edge. This finish will be at the back of the hat and should be in line with the short, straight section of braid at the beginning of the crown.

A little experimenting will prove that these instructions will cover almost any stitching problem as any construction is either flat or fulled. Even skirts may be made!

Chapter XI

BASKETS, FAVORS, FANS, MATS

WITH THE exception of the one-leaf basket, the items in the following instructions may be executed with other materials than the palmetto or palm fronds.

ONE-LEAF PALMETTO BASKET

This is an adaptation and a refinement of the onion baskets of Bermuda, which are made larger, more sketchily, and with a long, flat, braided handle to be worn across the forehead in order to balance the burden supported by the upper back. The foundation is a section of leaf midrib with double, unstripped fronds for spokes, so that it has all the natural strength of the palm leaf; consequently, even a very light lacing between the spokes produces a sturdy basket. Fig. 66AB.

Innumerable variations are possible and are limited only by the size of the leaf and one's imagination. Fashioning is not only simplified, but the appearance is improved if a dummy or form of the right proportions is available. A ten-inch-diameter crock with sharply turned sides is the ideal form over which to make a market basket, though a five-gallon water bottle makes a good substitute if a wooden

disk of the same diameter is placed in the basket under the bottle to correct its rounding edge. Good market-basket proportions are ten inches diameter by eleven inches to twelve inches high.

Not all palmetto fans are suitable basket leaves. In some the fronds will be too short, others too wide or too far apart on the leaf midrib. A leaf with long, medium-width fronds, Fig. 67, which have been separated for curing on the short divisions only, leaving the frond midrib intact so that the frond is double, should be selected. Lay back the half dozen or more small, butt-end fronds and choose sixteen to eighteen double fronds, depending on the width of the frond, in the best section of the leaf. Count the fronds on the other side of the leaf midrib to determine that there are the same number fronds on both sides, for the leaf sometimes grows more fronds on one side than on the other. This portion of the leaf must have the requisite number of double fronds on a section of leaf midrib not more than eight inches long, Fig. 68-*c-d*, in order to make it suitable for a ten-inch dummy. A longer section will pro-

FIGURE 66A. A group of one-leaf palmetto baskets varying in size from a small roll basket made of saw palmetto to a large laundry basket made of cabbage palmetto. These are made of one leaf each. Note the difference in the bottom of the small roll basket in Figure 66B and the larger basket on its side in Figure 66A.

trude beyond the edge of the dummy, and fewer fronds will result in a loose, open weave. Having determined the section of the leaf to be used, pull off the discarded butt-end fronds. Fig. 68-*a-b*. Pulling is better than cutting, as it leaves a clean stem. Cut off that part of the leaf midrib above the eighteen-frond section, Fig. 68-*c*, and saw off the leaf midrib about three fourths inch below the lower fronds. Fig. 68-*d*. Remove the beard or hair-

like fiber, Fig. 68-*e*, attached at the upper end of the frond midribs and soak this basket section with half of another leaf for an hour in cold water the night before it is to be used. Wrap in a heavy, wet cloth and allow to lie overnight for mellowing. Fronds cut away from the basket section may be used for weavers also; however, the most of those discarded are too small or too short to be used advantageously. The ideal weaver is a long,

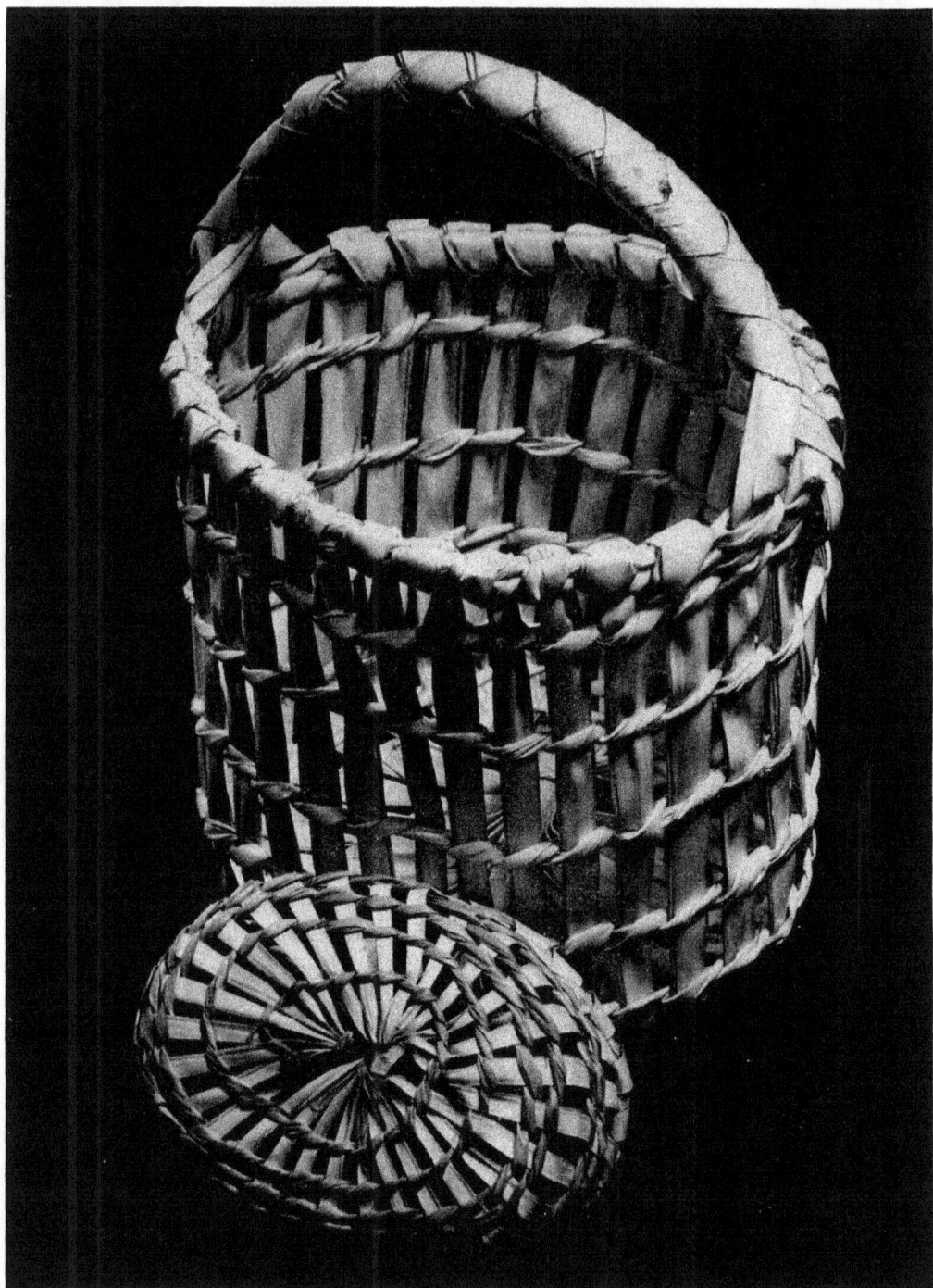

FIGURE 66B. Bottom of roll basket made of a leaf of saw or scrub palmetto and a sturdy, round-handled, one-leaf basket suitable for a shopping basket or fruit display. This is the basket described in the instructions herein.

narrow, double frond with all ribs left on.

Choose two such fronds which have been pulled from the leaf midrib (this allows a maximum length and is easier to use than a cut-off frond), trim butt ends only as much as necessary to get a sharp, one-sided point, Fig. 69-*a*, and tie together about three inches from their butt ends in a square knot. Fig. 69-*b*. Pull tight to make the knot as small as possible. Twist to form a neat coil, twisting these ends into the coil. Fig. 69-*c*. Slip one end of this coil under the midrib of the basket section, which has been laid on a table with the rounded side of the leaf midrib up; adjust the knot so that it lies to the left of the midrib between the sixth and seventh frond from the butt end. Fig. 69-*d*. Grasp both ends of the coil in the right hand, place the right forefinger between the coils, and push against them with it, at the same time pulling on the coils while making a half turn with the right hand, using an upward gesture, in order to cross them. Fig. 69-*e*.

Lay a double frond or spoke from the upper part of the section—that is, spoke No. 7 on the right—face up, in the V thus formed by the coiled weavers. Fig. 70. This will mean turning it over and back so that all frond midribs are toward the base. Hold weavers and spoke in place with the left thumb and forefinger, twist coils separately, cross them again, and lay in spoke No. 8. This is the familiar pairing weave, but has a handicap for the reed worker who has, of course, never had to give attention to the keeping of a symmetrical coil. A coil which has been twisted too tight is hard to handle and is more unsightly than one too loose. Twisting goes on constantly between the weaving of spokes. Proceed to the top of the leaf section in an easy oval, but, for the sake of future widening of the basket bottom, pair the two last spokes at the top on each side of the leaf midrib and treat them as one. Fig. 71-*a*. Proceed down the left side of the leaf midrib and pair two on each side as at the top, Fig. 71-*b*.

Splicing (Fig. 72)

When the weaver begins to seem small, cut another frond to a one-sided point and slip it between the double frond of the weaver to be spliced so that the point is behind a spoke which will help hold it. As the end of the old frond nears, wind the tips into the new coil.

Weaver Coils

Weaver coils must be kept at approximately the same size and at an equal tension; otherwise the weak weaver wraps around the strong one, or the loose around the tight one, spoiling the symmetry of the weave. Note, too, that there is no twisting of coils together, only a crossing between spokes of independently twisted weavers. There should be no twisting of coils together between spokes, only a *crossing* of the lower coil over the upper one. Figure 74

FIGURE 67. Material and tools required for one-leaf basket. The short full leaf is the basket leaf. The long slender part of a leaf is for the weavers. The saw is for cutting off end of leaf midrib; cord for reinforcing handle; ruler; carpet needle; punch stick; and clothespins. In addition to this, a pair of scissors will be needed.

FIGURE 68. Separation of fronds, *a*, where fronds were pulled off; *b*, fronds to be pulled off; ruler in position to determine the amount to be removed at top, *c*, and butt, *d*, to leave the maximum eight inches of length of midrib section which carries fronds best fitted for a basket; *e*, beard of hairlike fiber.

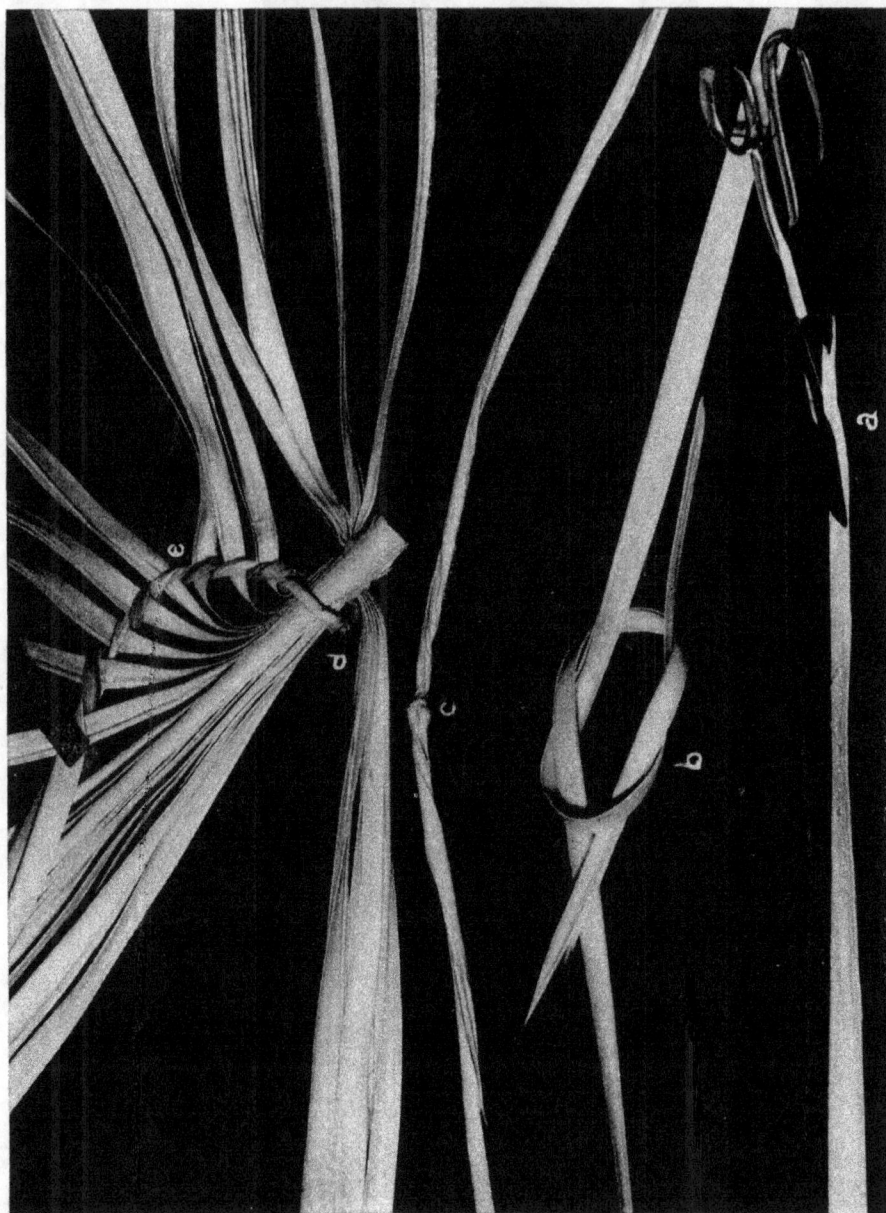

FIGURE 69. Detail showing, *a*, cutting end of weaver; *b*, making square knot; *c*, square knot tightened and ends rolled into weaver; *d*, knot placed at left of midrib; *e*, pairing weave made with two-color strand which shows the progress of the weave.

FIGURE 70. Pairing weave process, particularly laying the spoke or frond in the V formed by coiled weaver.

shows an example of the result of twisting the coils together between the second and third upright spokes, counting from the left. The unsightliness is obvious. Also this method locks the spokes in place so that any necessary adjusting is impossible.

Since the right forefinger is used steadily in twisting the coil or weaver, it is wise to protect it with a half-inch-wide band of adhesive tape put on

smoothly but not tight enough to bind. Place this band just below the base of the nail and around the finger, extending the wrapping down the finger midway between the first and second joints, as in Figs. 74 and 75 at x.

Weave the two unwoven fronds remaining on the right of the leaf midrib to complete the first row and lay the pattern. Place a spring clothespin on the weavers and the last spoke to

FIGURE 71. The completed first row with double frond left for future widening at top, *a*, and butt, *b*.

hold them and adjust the spokes. This is done by placing the thumb under each spoke where it branches from the leaf midrib and giving it a light push to arch it slightly. This relieves any strain and makes the spokes lie more evenly.

Swing out a little in spiral fashion

FIGURE 72. The new frond inserted into the old weaver at *a* and held by thumb ready for coiling.

and put in another row of pairing weave one to one-and-a-half inches from the first row, separating the fronds which were paired at the top, Fig. 71-*a*, and bottom, Fig. 71-*b*, when the first row was put in. Care should be taken to weave these in the order in which they grow on the midrib. Continue in an easy spiral until the diameter of the dummy has been built up. Fig. 73. Put in another row of pairing weave close against the diameter row, Fig. 73-*a*, center the dummy on the weave, and slip the second di-

FIGURE 73. Built-up base ready for the dummy; second row of pairing weave close to diameter row, *a*.

ameter row outward on the spokes. This will turn the spokes up against the sides of the dummy. Fig. 74. Adjust this row to about an inch from the base of the dummy and arrange spokes so that they stand at right angles to the base. They are inclined to drift to right or left if not watched. Weave in an easy spiral tightly against the dummy for ten and one half inches by measure all around in order to get the basket an even height. Put in another row of pairing close against the last in order to make a strong upper edge, Fig. 75-*a*, and fasten the ends

of the weavers by slipping them under a weave.

Choose four of the best fronds on right and left of the leaf midrib for the handle, Fig. 75-*b*. Measure to make certain of their position, which should be at right angles to the leaf midrib and over the center of the basket. Measure rather than count the spokes as the fronds will not be the same size. Mark these two groups of four each by pinning them together with a spring clothespin. This will hold them securely and will not injure them.

Adjust all spokes and take out any

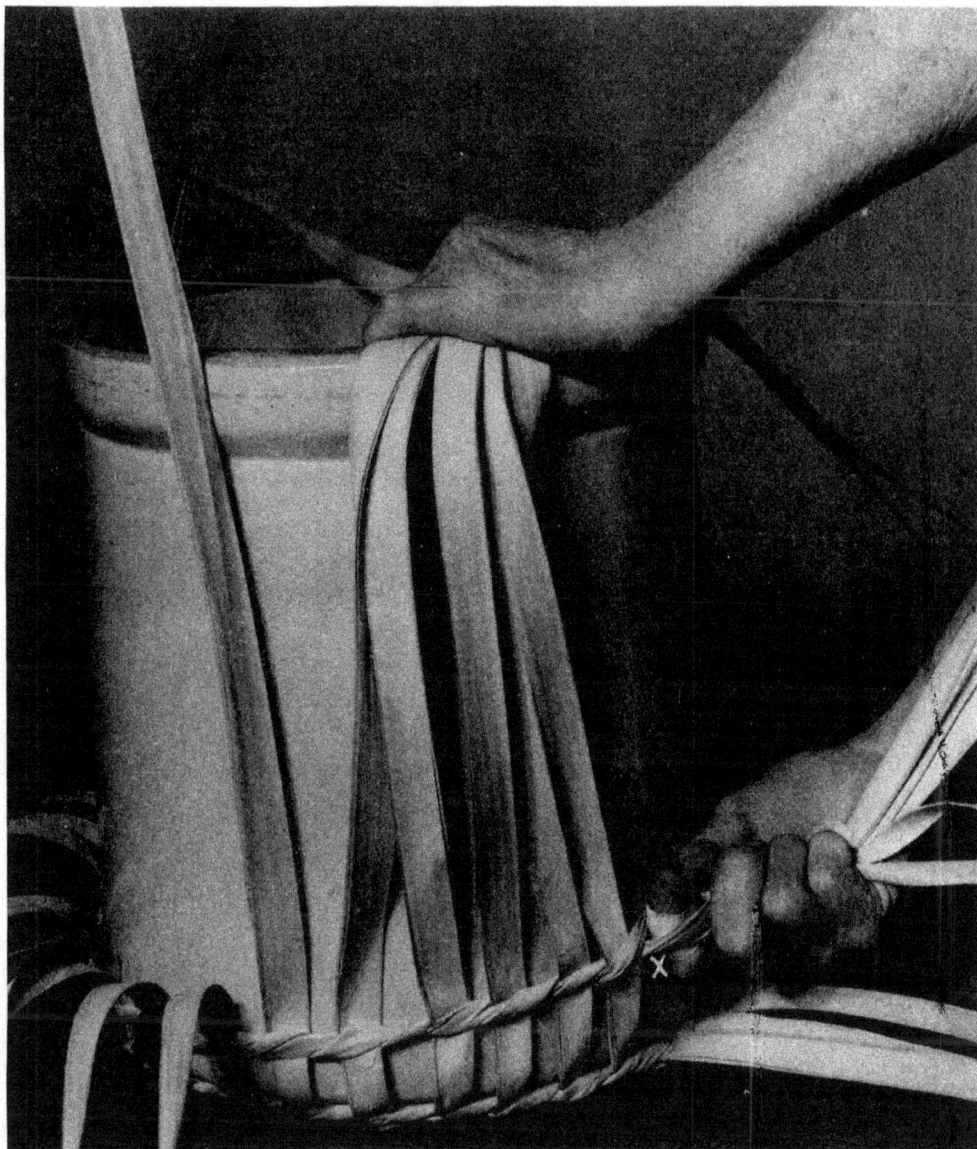

FIGURE 74. Turning of spokes up against the sides of the dummy.

looseness by pulling sharply upward on them; then remove the dummy. Grasp the top of a spoke to the right of a handle group with the fingers to the inside, tip of the thumb touching the top of the last pairing row, and make a sharp upward turn of the hand to give a triangular fold in the spoke. Fig. 75-c. With the left hand, hold this fold in place on the top and front of the last two rows of pairing, run the right hand to the tip of the spoke

FIGURE 75. Placing of row of pairing weave, *a*, close to last row to insure strong upper edge; *b*, choosing four best fronds on right and left of midrib for the handle; *c*, triangular fold made by spoke to make finished top.

FIGURE 76-*a*. Inserting punch stick for finishing edge; *b*, end of spoke frond after inserting behind two top rows of pairing weave and two other rows.

to be sure it is not twisted, and insert the end to the left below the two rows of pairing and between the spoke itself and the outer right handle spoke. Pull the frond through carefully and fit it snugly and neatly around the two rows of pairing.

Straighten the frond, and make a pocket in it by folding back the end for three or four inches into which put a well-smoothed, strong, slender stick about fourteen inches long with a square end. Fig. 76-a. Hold frond closely in place over the end of the stick and insert both behind the same spoke through the two top rows of pairing and at least two other rows. Fig. 76-b. Slip the stick and frond out between the spokes on the side of the basket, remove the stick and pull on the frond to tighten, and make a neat double loop on the upper edge of the basket. Continue around the basket until all spokes are finished individually in this manner except the two groups of four handle spokes on the sides.

The tips of the fronds are, of course, the most easily broken parts of the palmetto, so the ends must be well moistened if they are to stand up to the strain of inserting the frond between the spokes and the rows of pairing weave. Should they have become brittle, as is likely to be the case, by the time this point in the construction is reached, they should be soaked for about half an hour by inverting the basket over a pail of cold water so that all fronds and the upper edge of

the basket will be submerged. This will correct the condition. If the basket cannot be finished at one session, it may be treated like any other palmetto product and kept moist for forty-eight hours, after which it should be dried out to avoid souring. It may then be wet and the work taken up again.

Handle (Fig. 77)

To make a secure handle for a basket of this size, it must be reinforced with cord. Take a heavy, soft, twisted cord of about a yard in length, slip the ends under the two top rows of pairing between the second and third of the spokes which were reserved for the handle on each side. Bring the ends together and tie them with a square knot so that the length between the edges of the basket is sixteen inches, resulting in a double cord for both strength and padding. Adjust the cord so that the knot falls to one side of the center and trim the ends.

With moistened frond discarded from the basket leaf, build a core for a round handle by passing one end of a few fronds over one end of the cord just put in, under the two top rows of pairing; then turn up and tie the ends securely around cord and frond, Fig. 77-a, about three inches from the upper edge of the basket, using strong, lightweight twine. This will both cover the cord and furnish a filler for the handle. Slip the other end of this palmetto filler around the cord

FIGURE 77. Basket handle procedure: *a*, palmetto padding over cord and tied to conceal cord; *b*, *c*, *d*, beginning of four-strand handle weave.

at the other side of the basket, under the two upper rows of pairing, adjust smoothly, and tie.

Holding the basket between the knees, top toward the worker, cross the right inner spoke frond over the left inner spoke frond of one of the groups reserved for the handle, Fig. 77-b, and hold with the left thumb. Make an under turn, which is very nearly a right-angle turn, with the right outer spoke, and bring it snugly under the built-up core and the crossed center-spoke fronds to the outside and over the right inner-spoke frond, which is now on the left. Fig. 77-c. Make an under turn with the left outer-spoke frond and bring it around the core, under two and back over one. Fig. 77-d. Work from the right again under two and back over one. Tie securely and tighten the weave. Shred the loose ends of these fronds in order to make them lie closely and neatly together. Fig. 77-e. Tie firmly along the core at intervals of about two inches. Cut out any material unnecessary to the making of a core slightly under one inch in diameter, being careful to make it smooth and of equal size.

This handle procedure is identical with the round braid of Fig. 59B; hence it would greatly clarify the worker's understanding to first master that braid. The usual frond on the central part of a leaf section will be approximately one inch wide so that it will fit the core diameter specified above.

With the core made and one side neatly begun, the handle is ready for finishing. With the four unwoven strands, begin weaving the handle by crossing the right center-spoke frond over the left center-spoke frond.

Turn the right outer-spoke frond sharply under, weave under the core, under the crossed center fronds, and back over one. Turn the left outer frond sharply under, * Weave under the core, under two and back over one. Weave from the right under two and back over one.* Repeat procedure between stars (*).

Repeat this routine until the fronds begin to narrow, when they should be spliced with a single new frond. For durability, this should be split carefully so that the midrib remains on the half to be used.

Splice as necessary by placing the butt end of the new frond over the frond to be spliced and slipping it under a couple of checks in the weave. As it is narrower at the butt end, it will slip under the weave easily. Pull the frond back to take advantage of its best width, and pull all ends strongly to tighten the weave. Arrange all splicing to one side of the handle center, both for comfort and utility. Braid tightly to the other side of the handle, tightening frequently, and continue on over that part first woven so that the ends will fit neatly over the spokes. This will take a little planning.

Using the punch stick again, make a pocket in the end of the center frond which crosses over, and fit the frond neatly under the first two rows and two or more rows of pairing. Pull down firmly and smoothly. The other center frond is finished in the same way—that is, over the spokes—but the outer fronds may be put in either on the inner or the outer side of the spoke, depending on the position in which they fit best.

Trimming off of the ends of the fronds may be done as each spoke frond is woven back behind itself into the basket. However, it will save time and make any necessary adjustment of fronds possible if the trimming is done last and all at once. Cut off the fronds about one-half inch below the final pairing weave row through which the frond was slipped.

Variations

A particularly good flower-gathering basket may be fashioned from a very large leaf by using more spokes. Such a basket requires that the pairing weave be started near the middle of the leaf midrib and continued for approximately the same distance in all directions. A very large leaf will permit a distance of about nine inches, which would make an eighteen inch disk that should be finished in the same manner as the basket top or with the pointed edge described for table mats on page 119, under "Self-Point Finish," and in Fig. 82-c.

The spokes for the handles are chosen from the sides of the leaf midrib so that when the handle, which is the exact diameter of the disk, is

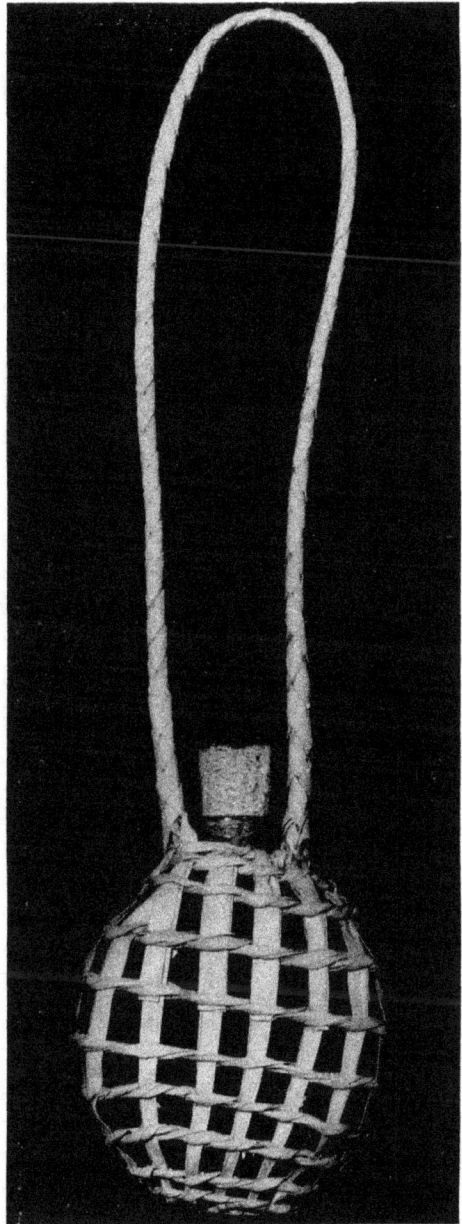

FIGURE 78. Juice bottle covered with scrub or saw-palmetto leaf in the one-leaf, basket-weave procedure. For use as a Girl-Scout canteen or flower holder. Corncob stopper.

picked up, the disk forms a half-round basket. When not in use, the basket lies flat. Size and method of making the handle are the same as for the market basket. However, the flat side of the leaf should be turned up for this basket.

Roll baskets should be made of the scrub or the saw-palmetto leaves, which are smaller. These "fans" have no leaf midrib, so that the pairing weave is begun by placing the coil around a group of about eight double fronds in the center of a leaf. There should be eight or ten double fronds on each side of the leaf below this group. As in the market basket, the rounded or underside of the leaf stem should be inside of the basket, as the front or upperside of the leaf will provide a flatter surface for the bottom of the basket.

Tie the butt ends of two long, thin, unstripped fronds together in a square knot. Twist into a coil in such a manner as to cover the ends. Pass one end of this coil under eight of the double center fronds about an inch from the end of the closely trimmed leaf stem. Using the pairing weave, lay the first of the eight spokes in the V so formed, cross the weavers again, and lay the second of the spokes in the V. Continue in this manner in an easy spiral until all spokes have been used and the point of beginning has been reached. Swing out for about an inch and put in another row of pairing weave. When the pairing is the approximate size and shape of the dummy, put in another row close

beside the last, center the dummy, and slip the last row of pairing about three-fourths inch outward on the spokes. This will turn up the spokes. Put in three or more rows of pairing weave around the dummy for the sides of the basket, the last two rows being put in very close together. Finish the top as described for the market basket.

The diameter of a roll basket is such that no widening is required at the top of the leaf as is necessary for the market basket; however, the fronds at the base of small leaves are of such size that it is sometimes desirable to allow for widening by grouping two double fronds on each side of the leaf stem and treating them as one. On the next row of pairing these should be separated so as to fill in a space that would otherwise be unsightly.

As in the market basket, straight spokes do not happen. They must be watched and made straight. Baskets with slanting or drifting spokes give the impression of a careless workman, and are second-rate products.

Good proportions are six inch by seven inch bottom and a height of two and one-half inches finished, though, as in all basketry, one's preference may rule.

COVERED SQUARE BASKET WOVEN OVER FORM
(Figs. 50-d and 79)

These instructions will adapt themselves to any size square basket if the width of the fronds used is such that an even number of weavers is used

both ways. A wide strand of about ½
inch was used for the basket in Fig.
50-*d* and a long strand, which held its
length without tapering and so did
duty on bottom and both sides without splicing, was secured by cutting
the frond to a half-inch measure. This
would not have been possible if the
strand had been stripped. Care should
be taken to measure from the straight
edge of the frond.

Work the fronds as lightly dampened
as possible, as this will insure a tight,
firm weave. There is no crease until
the edge of the basket is turned, so
very light dampening will suffice.
When the basket has been woven,
wrap it while still on the form in a
very damp towel for several hours
before turning the edge. This will
make it possible to turn the edge
strands without cracking them.

An excellent form or dummy is
made of a smoothly finished piece of
wood 4″ × 4 inches and 12 to 18
inches long, with a short piece of
board nailed across the end to hold it
erect. The extra length of the upright
takes care of the ends of the strands,
which become bothersome if they
have to be spread across the work-
table. For this reason, a crude form as
described above is superior to a cube.

Mark a true diagonal from corner
to corner, both ways, on the top of
the form.

Place a pair of strands of the longest
palmetto, one on each side of the
diagonal. Weave one over the other
at the corners as sketched and tie
down on the side with a soft string or

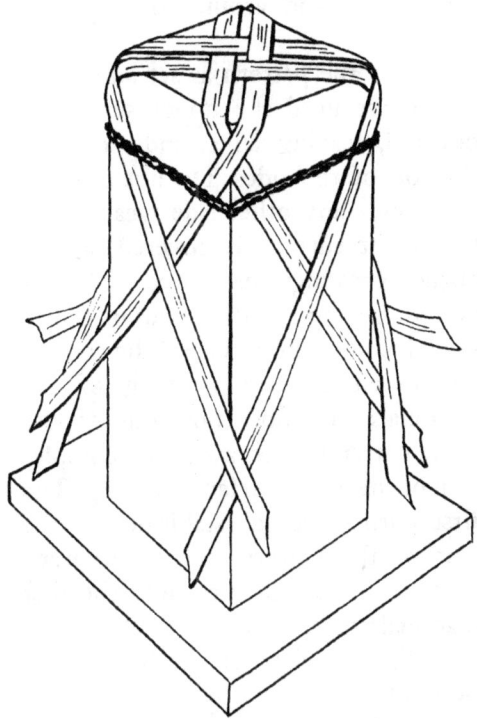

FIGURE 79. Covered square-basket procedure. This shows strands on the form
and method of weaving. The strands are
drawn out of proportion in order to give
the detail. Fig. 50-*d* shows the finished
basket.

a rubber band. The crossing at the
corners not only makes a square
corner but sets the pattern for all
strands to follow. The middle strands,
of course, are the longest, and those
toward the sides become successively
shorter.

Place another pair of strands one on
each side of the other diagonal and,
at the center, where the pairs cross,
weave over one, under one with one
strand, and under one, over one with
the other strand, crossing all corners
as illustrated and slipping the ends

under the band around the upright. Fig. 79.

Follow the pattern as set and fill in the weave until the upper surface is covered, leaving all strands loose at the top of the sides. Do not attempt to arrange any other side weave until the upper surface is covered, as the corner crossings may have to be reversed. Owing to differences in size of strand, size of dummy, and the routine established by the weaving of the diagonals, the final positions of the corner strands must await the completion of the upper surface weaving. The first corner weave establishes all the rest of the pattern. The temporary crossing is necessary to hold the first diagonals true. If they are allowed to side-slip, the edge of the basket will be slanted.

For the side weave, begin at a corner, make sure that the proper sequence of "over one, under one" is established, and weave around the four sides to the depth of an inch or more, fitting in corner sequences and continuing the weave around the sides as the progress of the weavers makes strands from other sides available.

When the sides have all been woven to the depth desired, tighten and true up. Dampen the basket as directed on page 109; then choose a pair of weavers where they cross and fold them upward. Crease and weave them back into the sidewalls for three or four checks to form a sturdy edge. When all sides of the edge have been woven, trim ends off close to a check

to make them not only invisible but to form a smooth surface for the cover.

For the cover, leave the basket on the dummy and weave another upper surface, following the instructions for the basket bottom. Weave the sides 1½ to 2 inches wide and finish as for basket.

For a firm, square, sturdy basket with straight edges, the diagonals must be kept true and the weave close.

PALMETTO-HORSE PLACE CARD AND FAVOR

(Fig. 80)

Select five strands about ⅛ inch wide. Grasp strand 1 between the thumb and fingers of the left hand about an inch from the butt, short end pointing toward the person. Arrange strand 2 midway its length over strand 1 and hold it with the left thumb and forefinger. Place strand 3 midway its length under strand 1. Lay strand 4 over strand 1, with the butt end extending about 2½ inches on the right. Lay strand 5 under strand 1 with the butt end extending about 2½ inches on the right. These short lengths extending on the right form the hind legs, the end of strand 1, the tail.

Weave under one, over one, under one with strand 2 on both right and left of strand 1. Weave under one, over one with strand 3 on both right and left of strand 2.

Grasp both ends of strand 2 and pull, to tighten the weave; sharpen the angles and square up. Pull in the same way on the ends of strand 3.

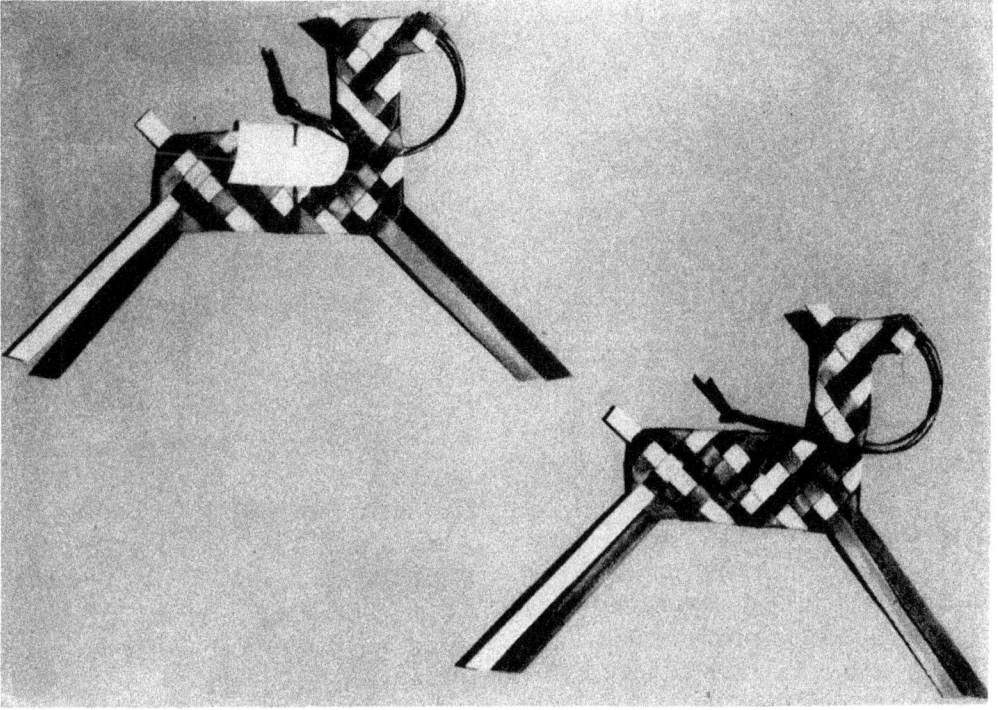

FIGURE 80. Place card and favor made of palmetto. When used as a place card, the name is written on the paper saddle. These are easy to make, low in cost, and amusing.

Weave under one, over one, under one, over one from the right. Weave again from the right, under one, over one, under one.

Weave alternately in this manner until there are six folds on the back or left, and seven folds under the belly. This will leave two strands on the right which will make the front legs. Drop these. Go over the work to tighten the weave and straighten the edges.

Turn under the right outer strand of the five remaining strands and weave it back to the left, under one, over one, under one, over one, in line with the upper part of the strand making the outer front leg, which brings the end of this strand out where the back joins the neck.

Weave again from the right, under one, over one, under one, and weave alternately from right and left, under one, over one, until there are five folds on the neck front, three folds on the neck back. This leaves three strands pointing right, two strands pointing left. These two last make the ears, so are dropped.

Weave under one, over one from the left. Weave again under one from the left. Weave under one from the

111

right. Weave under one from the left. This makes the three folds which form the top of the head.

Fold the single strand pointing left under two while holding the braiding very firmly (this movement is the most difficult of the entire construction) and weave the strand back over itself on the front so that the end comes out under the second head fold where it parallels the ear strands. Pull tight and cut close. This front underfold forms the nose, so is at an angle to the folds on the top of the head.

Fold the inner right strand under and back over itself—it being the second or middle fold on the top of the head—and run the end under one check of the weave to secure it. Pull tight and cut close.

Strip the remaining strand into three parts and trim off the upper one close to the nose. Have these strands long enough to loop gracefully for a bridle, and bring the ends to the back from each side of the neck. Tie together in a single knot and trim off the ends about ⅜ inch beyond the knot.

Trimming

Cut off ear strands about ⅛ inch above the top of the head, holding the scissors parallel with the top of the head.

Trim the back legs to approximately the length of the body, holding the scissors parallel with the body, and trim the front legs to match.

Trim the tail to about ¼ inch, cutting straight across the strand.

For a place card, cut a blanket of smooth paper folded to fit over the back of the horse. Fasten it on with a bit of thoroughly moistened waste palmetto stripped to about ¹⁄₁₆ inch width, and threaded from the underside through holes which have been made through the blanket near the center top by a single thrust of a large needle. Carry the end back through the second hole and tie the ends together firmly on the left side of the horse, preferably in a square knot. This leaves an adequate, clear space for the name.

Spread legs to make horse stand.

Care must be taken to place strand 2 *over* the tail strand so as to put the only flaw in the weave—made by the finishing off of the mouth strand—on the reverse side or left of the head. This makes all horses run to the right.

Pull all strands tight to make sharp-angle turns.

OTHER ANIMALS

A REINDEER may be made by splitting the ear strands and twisting them for horns, or, better, by cutting long, branching horns out of palmetto and inserting them behind the ears, which should be trimmed to a pointed roundness. The tail also should be similarly trimmed.

AN ELEPHANT may be made by using six wider strands to form a heavier body and finishing the head with a four-strand, round-braid trunk.

Make inserted ears and tusks by trimming two pieces of palmetto fan shape and slipping the pointed ends under checks on each side of the head. The handle or the pointed ends of the fan form the tusks and the bent-down fan shape forms the flop ears.

A GIRAFFE requires a shorter body and a longer neck. Leave tail one inch long and shred at the end.

A DOG needs shorter legs and flop ears, which may be inserted and bent down.

PALMETTO FAN IN PATTERN WEAVE WITH BAMBOO HANDLE
(Fig. 81-a)

Copied from a fan brought from Persia during World War II. Any combination of colors may be used, but to make the description of the weave clearer, the instructions are given based on colors green and brown, with an all-around section of natural.

Prepare twenty-five strands each of green and brown, and fifty-two strands of natural palmetto, a scant ¼ inch wide. The greater part of the natural strands will need to be less than 14 inches long so that one strand will furnish two or more weavers. Moisten lightly.

Mark a 9 inch square on a soft board which will take thumbtacks and is at least 15 inches square. This extra size is to allow the pinning of all strands three inches beyond the edge of the fan so that tack holes may be cut off when the strands are woven

back into the fan to make a selvedge.

Mark a true diagonal from corner to corner each way. Lay a strand of brown on this line from the upper left corner to the lower right corner and a strand of green from the lower left corner to the upper right corner, and pin them down at the edge of the board with thumbtacks.

Lay and pin down twelve of the brown strands on each side of the first strand laid, weaving in the strand of green which was crossed over the brown strand where the two diagonals met, under 3, over 3, under 3, over 3 on each side of the brown diagonal.

Make a band of green the same width as the band of brown by laying and weaving in twelve strands on each side of the green diagonal.

In order to secure the pattern of alternate brown and green diamonds as shown in the illustration, weave green into brown from left to right:
First row—under 1, over 3, under 3, over 3, under 5, over 3, under 3, over 3, under 1.
Second row—under 2, over 3, under 3, over 3, under 3, over 3, under 3, over 3, under 2.
Third row—under 3, over 3, under 3, over 3, under 1, over 3, under 3, over 3, under 3.
Fourth row—over 1, under 3, over 3, under 3, over 5, under 3, over 3, under 3, over 1.
Fifth row—over 2, under 3, over 3, under 3, over 3, under 3, over 3, under 3, over 2.
Sixth row—over 3, under 3, over 3,

FIGURE 81-*a*. Palmetto fan in pattern weave, with bamboo handle. This can be made of many other materials, and cane may be used for the handle. *b*. Fan made of pine needles in check weave, bound with palmetto braid and a round, braided palmetto handle. Written instructions for making this fan are not included. It is so simple, however, that it can be constructed by looking at the picture. *c*. Fan woven on the diagonal, using a section of palmetto leaf. *d*. Palmetto fan in pairing weave. This fan may be reproduced in any strong, pliable material.

under 3, over 1, under 3, over 3, under 3, over 3.

Seventh row—under 1, over 3, under 3, over 3, under 5, over 3, under 3, over 3, under 1.

Eighth row—under 2, over 3, under 3, over 3, under 3, over 3, under 3, over 3, under 2.

Ninth row—under 3, over 3, under 3, over 3, under 1, over 3, under 3, over 3, under 3.

Tenth row—over 1, under 3, over 3, under 3, over 5, under 3, over 3, under 3, over 1.

Eleventh row—over 2, under 3, over 3, under 3, over 3, under 3, over 3, under 3, over 2.

Twelfth row—over 3, under 3, over 3, under 3, over 1, under 3, over 3, under 3, over 3.

Weave in the other twelve green strands on the upper side of the center green diagonal, using this same sequence and working from the center upward. This will give a square of slightly more than four inches made up of alternate green and brown diamonds.

Weave in on each side thirteen strands of natural palmetto, following the pattern set. The procedure will be found easy once the routine of 5, 3, 1 at the points is established and understood. Push in tightly to center and square up.

Finish all edges by turning strands and weaving back into fan in such a manner as to preserve the color pattern. True up edges by lines drawn on the board to define size and shape of the fan. Trim off all ends neatly.

Handle

Secure a piece of well seasoned bamboo of about $\frac{1}{2}$ inch diameter and 20 inches long, preferably two joints. Saw off outside of the joint on each end. Smooth and polish.

Bore a $\frac{3}{16}$-inch hole through the upper end about $\frac{3}{4}$ inch from the end, and another in line with it about the same distance above the second or middle joint of the bamboo. Have these fully $9\frac{1}{2}$ inches apart.

Split the bamboo after tying firmly with twine above and below the holes to relieve strain and prevent splitting further than is necessary. Put a flat peg in the split to wedge it apart, and force one side of the well-moistened fan into the split, removing peg.

Select and thoroughly moisten three or four heavy, best-length strands of brown palmetto a scant $\frac{3}{8}$ inch wide, and fasten the end firmly at the upper end of the handle. Wrap around the bamboo handle twice, very firmly, and sew through the edge of the fan and around the handle with a whip stitch from the upper to the lower edge, splicing as necessary. Wrap the palmetto smoothly and firmly around the bamboo and sew it neatly through the weave of the fan.

Fasten the strand at the lower edge of the fan by wrapping it twice around the handle and then slipping the end back under the wrapping. Tighten and trim closely.

Remove the protecting twine ties around the bamboo at the upper and lower edges of the fan only after allowing fan to dry thoroughly.

FAN WOVEN ON THE DIAGONAL, USING A SECTION OF PALMETTO LEAF
(Fig. 81-c)

Choose a cabbage palmetto leaf with narrow fronds and a comparatively slender leaf midrib that carries nineteen fronds on approximately an 8-inch section. With the rounding outer side of the stem upward, trim ends off so as to have nine fronds on the left and ten fronds on the right of the stem. Leave fronds double.

Bring the first lower left strand under the leaf midrib to the front, and weave it over the second from the bottom frond to the right of the stem and under the first frond, where it may be held in place with a spring-type clothespin.

Bring the second frond on the left under the stem to the front and weave it over the third, under the second, and over the first fronds on the right of the stem. Fasten in place with a clothespin at the lower edge of the weave. The weaving of all nine fronds on the left of the stem in this manner will result in a triangular surface of about 6 inches.

To complete the fan, fill in to form an oblong of about 10½ inches length by 7½ inches width by turning over and upward ends 1 through 9, which were brought forward from the left side of the leaf midrib, and lay them parallel to the lower or first frond on the right of the stem and weave.

Fill in the upper right corner with fronds of similar size, pinning ends with clothespins.

Mark off a rectangle of the size determined upon, stitch along edges to be trimmed off on the upper and right sides, and trim to one-eighth inch of stitching.

Finish all raw edges with a binding of check-weave braid about one inch wide which has been moistened so that it may be folded in the center. Sew on by hand.

PALMETTO FAN IN PAIRING WEAVE
(Fig. 81-d)

Select twenty-four good heavy ribs taken from the middle of double fronds of the cabbage palmetto. Cut these to about 24 inches in length, measuring from the butt ends. This will give the heaviest part of the rib for the spokes over which the pairing is to be made. Lay these so that twelve butt ends point to right and twelve to the left. This will equalize the size of the ribs to some extent.

Beginning at a point nine inches from the left end of these bundled ribs, wrap them firmly toward the right end with a strand of palmetto ¼ inch wide for a distance of 6 inches. Wrap closely so that edges of the strand touch but do not overlap.

Bring the ends of the wrapped section together and tie securely with a strong, fine twine. This forms a loop, which is the fan handle.

Divide the ribs into three groups and weave from side to side in pairing weave. This procedure is described in detail in the directions for the one-leaf basket. See page 93 and Figs. 69-e and 70. Weave from left to right, turn the fan over, arranging the selvedge neatly, and weave from left to right. By this method, the fan has no distinct front and back. After six rows have been put in, subdivide the spokes into six groups and weave in six rows. Press down firmly.

Subdivide the spokes into twelve groups and weave in twelve rows of pairing.

Subdivide into twenty-four spokes of two ribs each and put in about thirty rows of pairing weave. Press down firmly.

This will give an overall woven surface of about 8 inches high by 12 inches wide. Size, of course, will vary with width of strand and firmness of weave.

Splicing is accomplished by laying the butt of the new strand under the old tip and twisting them lightly together, when they may be treated as if they were one.

To secure the corners, which are the points of weakness, moisten the ends of the spokes thoroughly to make them pliable and lay them along the top of the last row of pairing weave. Catch these down with firm but widely spaced over-and-over stitches. It adds to the durable qualities of the fan if all spokes are so fastened down.

Cover this edge with a check-weave braid of less than one inch width, folded to make a binding, and stitch invisibly and firmly.

Moisten fan lightly, pull into shape, and put under press to dry.

Color scheme is a matter of individual preference.

WOVEN MATS
(Fig. 82)

These are useful, decorative and substantial, and may be used for luncheon mats, hot plates, and for under flowerpots and vases. They are washable and wear well and, in case of a break, mend beautifully.

Tools required are a supply of thumbtacks—for the ends of all fronds need to be fastened down—and a board of wood soft enough to take the tacks easily. The board should be 5 inches larger on all sides than the mat. This will allow for pinning the fronds down at the edge of the board so that the one-inch allowance for points and the two inches of strand for weaving back into the mat to effect a firm edge will be provided. The part of the frond blemished by the tack holes may be trimmed off.

Width of strand is a matter of preference. Strands of $\frac{1}{4}$ inch and less should be stripped in the usual manner. If, however, a strand width of $\frac{3}{8}$ to $\frac{1}{2}$ inch is desired, the maximum sustained width and consequently longer strand may be obtained only by cutting the frond to a measure. In preparing a wide strand, much width toward the tip of the frond is lost by stripping, due to the fact that the frond is made up of tapering fibers along which it naturally strips. Cutting is not advisable for $\frac{1}{4}$-inch and narrower strands. It is, in fact, wasteful for such widths, both in time and material.

Decide upon the size of the mat. Using a true edge, draw the measurement on the board, having it well centered. Then draw a second rectangle inside the first and just the width of the strand to be used from the edge of the first rectangle; *i.e.*, if the strand is to be ½ inch wide, make the second or inner rectangle line ½ inch inside the first on all sides. The inner line is the weaving line, the outer one the point guide. The mat may be made up of any width strands, but if self-finish points are to be used, there must be an even number of strands both on width and length, and the strands must be of approximately the same width as the turning of the point necessitates the weaving in of each strand on the adjacent one.

Grade for length and put aside the longest strands for the horizontal weavers. Strands at this stage of the weaving should be worked as dry as possible in order to avoid swelling of the fibers and a consequent unsightly, open product when they dry out.

Pin the shorter strands across the long edge of the rectangle, fastening the upper ends down firmly with tacks at the edge of the board. Fill in the entire inner rectangle, laying the strands close together at the outer rectangle line to prevent spaces showing between, but do not overlap. Fasten down the ends at the edge of the board as they fall; owing to the tapering of the strands, they will not be close together at the edges of the board.

Put into the board at the upper corners of the inner rectangle and along its upper edge between the strands at intervals, a row of dress pins. These will act as guide lines and firming agents for the horizontal weavers, which are now ready to be put in.

Lift the lower end of all uneven-number strands and lay in the first long weaver. Place the edge against the row of pins, and fasten both ends down firmly with thumbtacks on the edge of the board.

Lift all the even-number strands and lay in the second weaver. Push up firmly. Pin down both ends near edge of the board. Keep right and left edges true to the inner rectangle lines.

This is an overall "over one, under one" or check weave, which is the simplest and most adaptable form of mat making. Fig. 82-*a-b*. Proceed, using alternate weavers until the entire surface of the mat, except for the outer left and right rectangle lines, is covered. The weave should be made tight as it is worked; however, some extra tightening will be found necessary, and for this purpose the eraser of a pencil will save one's fingers and do a better job of pushing strands together.

As the self-points require a sharp crease, it will be well to spread a thoroughly moistened towel over the work at this point. After an hour or so, the strands will be sufficiently pliable to crease without breaking. Remove a tack from a strand which is woven over by the horizontal weaver, trim it on a slant near the end so that it may be entered more easily into the weave, and for the self-points proceed as follows:

Self-Point Finish (Fig. 82-c)

Beginning on one side of the mat, turn every other strand, first as at *1*, then as at *2*, and weave end of turned strand back into the mat so a clean point is left, as at *3*. When alternate strands have been turned in this manner all around the mat, turn the mat over and proceed in the same way with all remaining strands. The ends of the turned strands are woven into the mat and thus hidden under one of the weavers and trimmed off close to the check.

Turned-in Edges

Another and easier method of making mats, demanding less patience, time, and artistry, provides for the use of narrower-stripped fronds of unequal width. These are evened up to a very satisfactory degree by placing butt and tip alternately. As the edge is finished by turning each end over on itself, the inequalities present no hazard. Also, as there are no points, the turn-in allowance may be shorter. The same rectangle drawing may be used, observing the outer line as the turn line.

Grade strands for length. Fasten down the upper end of the shorter strands, as previously described, and weave in the longer strands. Tighten and fasten down the long strands as the weaving progresses.

When the entire rectangle is covered and tightly woven, select an end which lies under the horizontal weaver, trim the end to a one-sided point for ease in inserting, and weave it back on itself for about an inch and a half to make a firm edge. Proceed around the mat, weaving every other strand until all sides have been woven. Tighten and trim off closely.

Remove all remaining thumbtacks, turn the mat over, weave all unwoven ends, tighten, and trim.

Bound or Braid-Edge Finish

Edges may be finished by turning and weaving in half of the strand ends on each side to hold the weaving secure, removing all thumbtacks, and trimming the rest of the strand ends close to the sides of the mat. A binding of cloth, tape, oilcloth, or braid will give good service for this type of finish.

A decorative band of four-strand fishtail, rickrack, or some of the plain braids makes an attractive finish, particularly if the braid is woven from color and the mat is of natural palmetto. An example of this treatment is shown in Fig. 82-*a*. Turn the corners just as if mitering cloth braid or binding.

Diagonal Weave

Mats to be used in making handbags and brief cases work more easily and have less tendency to break if they are woven on the diagonal. This

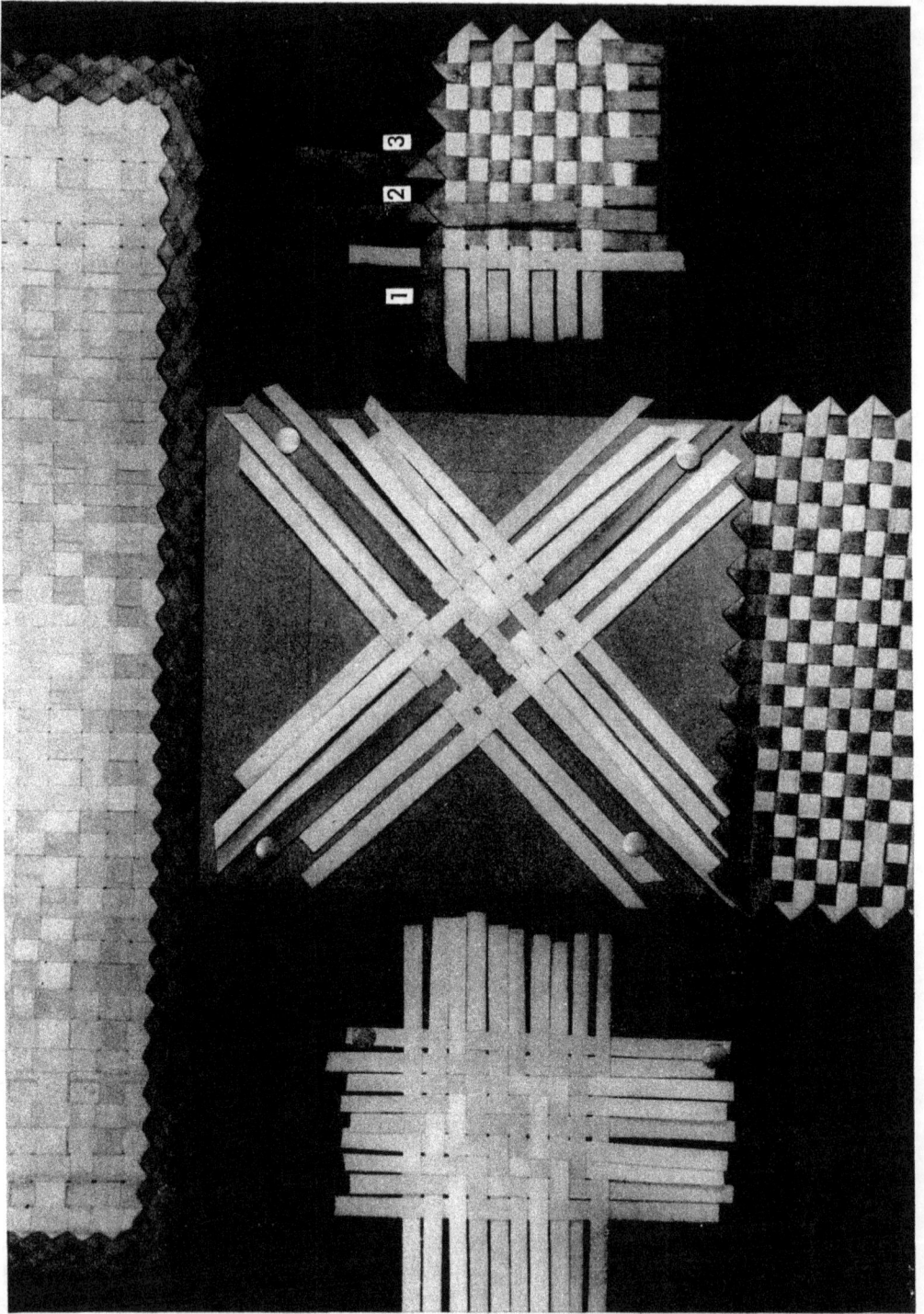

FIGURE 87 Square *k* [?]

120

weave also makes an attractive pattern for mats and lends itself to elaboration.

On the rectangle drawn on the board for check-weave mats, lay off on the left end an exact square, by measuring and marking on the upper and lower horizontals for a distance equal to the width of the rectangle. Draw a line from upper to lower horizontals at this measure to indicate the square.

Draw diagonal lines from corners to corners of this square. Fig 82-d. Lay a weaver on each diagonal line, centering them and fastening to the board securely with thumbtacks. These strands are the guidelines for the rest of the mat. Fig. 82.

Weave in check pattern, filling in on right and left, above and below, covering the entire surface of the rectangle.

A finished edge may be made by turning a strand over on the rectangle line and, on the angle at which it fits, weaving it back into the mat. At the tips of the corners, the strands will weave back on themselves; and, for several strands on each side of the corners, the strands must be turned twice and fitted closely around side and end.

If preferred, this too may have the weave secured by weaving in a few strands on each side, the size marked, and the edge machine-stitched, trimmed closely, and bound—or, in the event cattail rush or other soft fiber is used, by putting about three rows of machine stitching around the edges, after lengthening the stitch and loosening the tension.

Twill Weave

This is the regular twill weave seen in baskets from all parts of the world. Proceed as directed for the check-weave mat through fastening down of the upper ends of the shorter perpendicular strands. Strands for this weave may be any width preferred. See Fig. 82-e.

* Beginning at the pattern edge and working from right to left, weave in a long strand, under one, over two, under two, continuing across the entire mat in alternate "over and under" pairs, and pin the ends of this horizontal weaver down near the edges of the board.

Weave over two, under two across the mat surface with a second horizontal weaver in alternate "over and under" pairs. Push in well to tighten, and pin down the ends of the weaver near the edges of the board.

With a third strand, weave over one, under two, over two, weaving in alternate "under and over" pairs across

FIGURE 82. Samples of mat weaves. *a.* Check-weave mat finished with four-strand fishtail braid sewed around the edge. This mat is size 12½ by 22 inches, very fine for the dining table. *b.* Check-weave mat in two colors with self-finish point edge. *c.* Detail of folding the strands for the self-point finish. *d.* Detail of laying the strands for the weaving of the diagonal-weave mat. *e.* Detail of pattern of twill-weave mat.

all perpendicular strands. Tighten weave and pin down ends.

With a fourth long strand, weave under two, over two in alternate "under and over" pairs across the perpendicular strands. Push up the weave closely and pin down the ends of the horizontal weaver.*

This gives the entire, allover twill sequence. Repeat procedure between stars (*) to fill in the rectangular pattern on the board. Finish as in straight-edge mats.

Keep edges true and the weave close.

The variations of this weave are limitless, as even a little experimenting will show.

INDEX

Trimming bands (*cont'd*)
four-strand round, 74, 75
in color, 81
push-and-pull, details and sample of, 71,
73, 74
rickrack, details and sample of, 71, 73
three-strand, details and sample of, 70, 71,
72
two-strand, details and sample of, 70, 71
Twill weave, 120, 121, 122
Twin-curl
combination, with double-strand scallop,
details and sample of, 47, 48, 49
herringbone, with single-strand scallop,
details and sample of, 45, 47, 48
Turned-in edges for mats, 119

U

Uneven-strand check-weave braiding, 22, 24–
26

W

Weaver coils, tension of in basketry, 93
Weaving
baskets, 90–110
mats, 117–122
Weaving samples, for mats, 120
Wetting palmetto, 9, 21

Y

Yucca, varieties of, 10, 12